BO

HE WAS EVERY PARENT'S NIGHTMARE

*"When the woods are black as night
That's the bogeyman's delight.
Better run away, better run away
Pretty little maiden run away."*
-- Author Unknown

STEVE JACKSON

WILDBLUE
P R E S S

WildBluePress.com

Some names have been changed to protect the privacy of a few of the individuals discussed in this book. Also, some conversations are recollected from the memories of characters in the book and presented as quoted dialogue for dramatic purposes; efforts were made, however, to corroborate the accuracy and context of the conversations.

As with any book comprised of the blending of a number of individual stories, some personal accounts received more attention and space than others; other worthwhile accounts do not appear at all. The author may have decided to use one account over another as representative of others, but the intention was not to slight the importance of events on any individual or group. The "ripples in the pond" caused by David Penton washed over far more people than this book can record.

Other WildBlue Press Books by Steve Jackson

Smooth Talker
http://wbp.bz/st

No Stone Unturned
http://wbp.bz/nsu

BOGEYMAN *published by:*
WILDBLUE PRESS
P.O. Box 102440
Denver, Colorado 80250

WILDBLUE PRESS is registered at the U.S. Patent and Trademark Offices.

978-0-9905573-0-2   *Mass Market Paperback ISBN*
978-0-9905573-1-9   *eBook ISBN*

Interior Formatting by Elijah Toten
www.totencreative.com

Acknowledgements

The author wishes to express his grateful appreciation first to the law enforcement officers who participated in the writing of this story, especially Gary Sweet, Bruce Bradshaw, and Jeff Heck. And more than their help with this work, I'd like to thank them, as well as other officers such as Bob Holleman and Jerry Schrock who have passed on, for their quiet, often unappreciated and unrewarded, service to the people they take an oath to serve and protect. Far too often the only notice the men and women in law enforcement receive is when a "bad apple" makes headlines, but those individuals do not represent the vast majority who accept the dangers, hardships and stress and do their jobs well on behalf of their communities. There are dragons in the world, and we should be thankful that there are also dragon-slayers.

I would be remiss if I didn't note the considerable contributions of the spouses of some of the detectives to this book so that we may appreciate from their unique perspectives the dedication and sacrifices their husbands make; the families also make sacrifices. So thank you Julie Sweet, Gail Bradshaw and Molly Robertson.

I would also like to thank my extraordinarily talented editor, Jenni Grubbs, and my partner at WildBlue Press, Michael Cordova, without whose expertise, extraordinary efforts and belief in this brave, new world of indie publishing, this story and the others found at WildBluePress.com might have never seen the light of day.

Lastly, I wish to thank the people in my life who make all the work, long hours, and absences worth it. First are my family starting with my parents, Donald and Charlotte, whose love, belief in me, and encouragement has never wavered; my sister, Carole, her husband, Bob, and my nephew, Michael, who supported me not only with their love but with shelter from the storm; my sister, Mary, who makes me laugh; and my much-missed brother, Donald, who reminds me of what it means to be a good man, a good brother, and a good son. A special tummy rub for Winkie the Wonder Dog—some might wonder why I'd want to acknowledge a crazy, sometimes frustrating canine, but in the hardest and loneliest times of my life, he has been my big-hearted companion. I also count on the love and support of my children, Mackenzie, Hannah and Lillia, and their fine, young men, Eric and Iaian; and my newest reminder that there is no bottom to the well of love, my grandson Callum. I also thank Roger, Patti, Doug, Linda, Brian, Tom, Kathy, Tim, and Carla; I am so grateful that when I need someone to talk to, a shoulder to cry on, a beer or a kick in the ass, you are there. And last, never least, my companion Janet Roll, without whose love and support these past few years, I would have been truly lost but instead am truly happy, there are no words to express my gratitude and love.

If the measure of a man's worth is the people who love him and are loved in return, then I am wealthy beyond all measure.

He stands on the edge of a foul dark pond as the cold winds of hell howl around him. In his cruel hands, he holds a collection of shiny pebbles that represent every child he took, subjected to unspeakable horrors and pain, and then remorselessly killed in the most terrifying manner imaginable. With each murder, the monster, this bogeyman, this nightmare, tosses a pebble into the bottomless waters causing ripples of misery and devastation to spread outward, engulfing his victims, their families, friends, police officers, communities, and even, as these sorts of beyond- the-pale atrocities becomes public knowledge, the national consciousness. They erode how secure we feel in our homes, how safe our children are playing in the yard, whether evil is winning the battle...

PART I

Every Parent's Nightmare

CHAPTER ONE

January 19, 1985

After several days of cold, the weather on that Saturday in Mesquite, Texas, had turned downright balmy, with bluebird skies and temperatures climbing into the mid-seventies. Many of the town's citizens were out enjoying the sunshine in the parks, playing softball, and watching their kids laughing and chasing each other on the playgrounds. Others used the opportunity to go for a drive in the countryside around Mesquite, a satellite city fifteen miles due east of Dallas.

Detectives Bob Holleman and Bruce Bradshaw were home with their families enjoying a quiet Saturday afternoon when they got the call about 3 p.m. It was a moment that would forever alter the partners' lives, though in drastically different ways.

Holleman was watching television with his wife, Molly, and their seven-month-old daughter, Emily, when the phone rang and he picked up. He listened with a frown, then Molly heard him say, "Well keep me updated," before he set the receiver down. Thirty minutes later, the phone rang again. This time he asked her to hang it up after he walked back to his home office. When he returned, he was dressed for work. "Looks like we've got a child abduction; they think it's the real thing. … I don't know when I'll be home."

Molly understood. A seven-year veteran with the Mesquite Police Department, her husband worked with Bradshaw in the Crimes Against Juveniles unit. Most of these calls about missing children turned out to be false alarms; the child would be found at the neighbor's or playing in a field and handled quickly. Occasionally, a parent locked in a custody battle took, or didn't return, a child, but those cases were usually resolved within a few hours.

After five years of marriage to a cop, especially a dedicated officer like her husband, Molly was used to the long hours and sudden calls to work when other families would be enjoying their weekends and holidays off. So she had no way of knowing that in a very real sense, their lives had been changed forever by a stranger.

Bruce Bradshaw was also enjoying an afternoon off with his wife, Gail, and their two daughters, Jodi and Laci, ages three and one, when Holleman called him. A little girl was missing from an apartment complex over near Highway 80, a main thoroughfare that runs east to west through Mesquite. He didn't give a lot of other details, but Bradshaw could tell from his partner's voice that he was stressed. "I need your help," Holleman said.

Bradshaw sighed and went to change his clothes. Their lieutenant, Larry Sprague, insisted that they dress professionally in a suit and tie whenever they were called out. Properly attired, he kissed his wife and headed for the door.

Gail watched him go and expected that he'd be home in time for dinner. Sometimes people asked her if it was hard saying goodbye to Bruce when he'd leave for work because of the dangers inherent with the job. She'd answer that it was really no different than when their spouses went to work, except that her husband was fully aware of the evil he might face and carried a gun for protection. No, she'd say, the hard part wasn't watching him go; it was learning to live with the darkness he sometimes brought back home with him.

Bradshaw had been born and raised in Comanche, a small farming and ranching community in central Texas. His core values and strong Christian faith were instilled in Comanche. He'd grown up inspired by John Wayne westerns, the Lone Ranger, and other tales from the Old West in which justice prevailed and the bad guys paid for their crimes. An uncle who'd been a deputy sheriff, William McCay, influenced his career choice. McCay was what you'd picture an old-time Texas lawman to look like: tall in the saddle—a former ranch hand, he was good with a horse—and always dressed in a cowboy hat and boots. Such was his influence that Bradshaw, his brother, and three cousins all ended up in law enforcement, a job that Bradshaw saw as an ongoing battle between good and evil.

Bruce met Gail, a Dallas native, when they were both attending Tarleton State University in Stephenville. Tarleton was a small "cowboy" college with a good science program. Perfect for a small town boy who'd never been on an escalator until Gail took him to a mall after he got the job with the Mesquite Police Department.

As he drove to meet up with his partner, Bradshaw, a medium-built man with intense hazel eyes behind thick-rimmed glasses and a bushy reddish moustache, also thought he'd be back in a couple of hours. However, this bright and shiny day was about to turn dark.

Arriving at the Charter Oaks apartment complex in a lower-middle-class, residential neighborhood, Bradshaw met up with Holleman, who briefed him on what was going on and what he'd learned from the witnesses so far. The call for help had come from Linda Meeks, the distraught mother of five-year-old Christi Meeks. She'd tearfully explained that she was divorced and that her daughter and son, Michael, age seven, were visiting for the weekend. She'd been inside the apartment getting supper ready when Michael and a nine-year-old neighbor girl named Tiffany Easter ran in to tell her that Christi had gone off with a stranger.

As they were talking, Lt. Sprague and their sergeant, Maggie Carathers, arrived and were also briefed. They called in more detectives and began assigning them to start canvassing the neighborhood. Meanwhile, Bradshaw was tasked with talking to Michael Meeks and Tiffany Easter.

Traumatized, Michael wouldn't say much. However, Tiffany was more forthcoming. She said the three of them were roller-skating on the sidewalk when a young white man approached. She described him as about the same height as Bradshaw, around five-foot-ten, a hundred sixty pounds, with medium-length brown hair and bangs, unshaven, possibly with a moustache. He was wearing a pullover shirt, shorts, and tennis shoes.

Tiffany said he asked if they'd like some cookies. Older and more wary, she tried to get her two younger friends away from the man by inviting them to her house; she said she had cookies, too. Michael followed her, but Christi stayed behind.

Meanwhile, Holleman located two young Hispanic boys in the building south of where Christi was last seen. They claimed that they saw Christi get into a car with a man. The car was small, they said, but couldn't agree on whether it was yellow or gray.

The detectives knew that Christi was in danger. But these were the days before cell phones, Amber Alerts, and the internet, so all they could do to get the word out to other law enforcement agencies was send a statewide teletype. They were also starting to worry about a change in the weather. A 'blue norther,' a swift-moving cold front named for its gunmetal-blue sky and cold winds, was racing in from the north. Within minutes, the temperature dropped thirty degrees, and the searchers worried that the stranger might let the little girl go somewhere in a rural part of the county where she'd be exposed to the elements wearing only a "Color Me The Rainbow" T-shirt, blue jeans, and Cabbage Patch Doll shoes.

More officers were called in to help search nearby parks, fields, and drainage ditches. But as night fell and temperatures plunged, there was no sign of Christi or the man who'd taken her. Bradshaw and Holleman drove home to dress in warmer clothes, but other than a quick word with their families, they were soon back out knocking on doors. Yet, despite the number of people who'd been outside the day before, they couldn't find anyone else who'd seen anything suspicious. They also drove past all of the motels and hotels in the area looking for a car that matched the description of the suspect's vehicle.

Members of the community volunteered to help, and the search widened, including by aircraft. Photographs of the little girl with brown eyes and sandy-blonde hair—possibly wearing a gold necklace with a red stone in the middle of a heart—were distributed. But she'd simply vanished.

The process of elimination began with the detectives asking the immediate family to take lie detector tests to remove them from suspicion; both parents passed. Christi's father, Mike Meeks Sr., was tough to deal with;

he angrily blamed his ex-wife for letting Christi out of her sight and as the days passed, constantly called the detectives demanding updates, though there was little they could say.

A reward generated telephone calls and leads to follow. Psychics contacted the police to offer their help or claiming to have some other-worldly information. The days turned into weeks, and then two months passed with nothing concrete to go on.

In March, a young man named Bruce Greene, a graduate of the Art Department at the University of Texas, called the Mesquite Police Department and said that perhaps he could sit down with Michael Meeks and Tiffany Easter and create a composite drawing of the suspect. The two children were brought to his art studio, where they described the young white male with longish dark hair, parted in the middle, and pale blue eyes set below a wide forehead.

Posters were made of the composite and distributed around town, as well as given to the news media. The drawing caused a new flurry of "tips," which the detectives had to record and then track down.

In 1985 there was no such thing as a sex offender registry, so Holleman and Bradshaw developed a priority system for leads. If a person called in and had pertinent information or knew of someone who looked like the composite and also had a history of committing sex crimes, they gave the lead a Priority One status. If the information was less pertinent to the investigation, they assigned it as a Priority Two. If the caller simply thought they knew someone who looked like the composite but had no other information, it was Priority Three. There were no computers for filing their information, so they kept a card file to cross-reference the leads by hand. But none of the tips led to Christi or her abductor.

Then on April 3, two fishermen spotted what they at first thought was a large dead bird floating in a cove of Lake Texoma, a sizeable body of water seventy-five miles north of Mesquite on the border of Texas and Oklahoma. However, on closer inspection the fisherman realized, to their horror, that the "bird" was a dead child.

Found below a cliff in a remote, heavily wooded area of the lake, the body had been in the water for a long time and was badly decomposed. In fact, the justice of the peace initially called in to identify the remains, believed them to be that of a boy. A few days later, the body was delivered to a medical examiner's office; the ME then called the Mesquite Police Department with a different story. He said the body belonged to a little girl, and she might be their missing child. She was wearing a Cabbage Patch Doll shoe, blue jeans, and a "Color Me The Rainbow" T-shirt.

These were the days before DNA testing, so Bradshaw called Christi's father, Mike, and told him that the body of a young female had been found in Lake Texoma and she might be his daughter. He said they needed to locate dental records for Christi, if they were available, to make a positive identification. Christi's father told him how to find her dentist, who reported to the medical examiner's office and confirmed everyone's worst fear: The dead child was Christi Meeks.

At the same time, Christi's family also reported to the medical examiner's office to identify her clothing. Holleman went with them.

In one way, finding Christi's remains was a relief. At least her parents didn't have to wonder if she was still out there somewhere, terrified and alone with the mysterious bogeyman who'd taken her. She could be given a proper burial. Still, there was no closure; not for her family or the lawmen assigned to find her killer.

Bradshaw and Holleman, along with several other officers from the Mesquite Police Department, attended the funeral, writing down license plates and photographing the crowd at the funeral on the possibility that the suspect might be there. They then watched the gravesite for several days afterwards, stopping people who visited the grave and asking for their identification. Many citizens dropped by to leave items such as flowers, stuffed animals, cards, letters, and even the lyrics to the John Denver song, "Rhyme and Reasons."

> *"So you speak to me of sadness*
> *And the coming of the winter*
> *Fear that is within you now*
> *It seems to never end."*

The detectives collected many of the items brought by mourners and tried to lift fingerprints so they could identify the visitors. But if the suspect attended the funeral or left behind some token of his presence, they couldn't find proof of it, and the questions remained. What sort of monster could have done such a thing to an innocent little girl? Was he a member of the community? Or was he a stranger, just passing through as he carried out his depredations?

The questions became an obsession for Holleman and Bradshaw. But of the two, Bob took it to another level and paid a price for it. The husband Molly Holleman watched walk out of the door following what she came to think of as "The Call" never came home again—at least not as a whole man.

The first night, he'd returned home just long enough to put on warmer clothes, but over the next few days Molly hardly saw him at all. She was working, and he was coming back to the house only long enough to grab a few minutes on the couch, shower, and put on clean clothes before he was gone again. But his clothing wasn't all that changed; his personality did, as well.

When they met and married in 1980, Bob was funny, witty, a real gentleman, and the smartest man she would ever know, constantly hungry for knowledge. Born and raised in Dallas, he'd always wanted to be a physician and even after becoming a police officer continued to take classes towards eventual entrance to med school through the University of Texas. College textbooks were his choice when reading for pleasure.

He also loved being a cop and never missed a day or shirked an off-duty call. He cared about people and was well-regarded by his peers and supervisors as a detective and the department's hostage negotiator. When he went to work, he always smiled and told Molly, *"Time for me to go crush some crime."*

Away from the job, he was a loyal friend, a loving husband, and, after Emily was born in May 1984, a dedicated father, who insisted on taking the 4 a.m. feedings and made sure he read to her at bedtime every night he was home. He couldn't carry a tune in a bucket, but he would rock his daughter to sleep singing *"The Battle of New Orleans"* as a lullaby.

"In 1814 we took a little trip,
along with Colonel Jackson down the mighty Mississip.
We took a little bacon and we took a little beans,
and we caught the bloody British in the town of New Orleans."

The Call changed all of that. From that moment forward, he was totally consumed by what happened to Christi Meeks. Every waking moment he was thinking about the case, going over and over the facts, searching for something they'd missed. If a lead came up, he'd run it to the ground until he'd exhausted all possibilities. He spent a lot of time with Christi's parents, especially Mike Meeks. Molly always thought it was because as a father, he identified with the other man's suffering. As such, he witnessed the horror the other family was going through and felt guilty because he was helpless to do anything about it. The formerly life-loving detective slowly began to withdraw and grew morose and gloomy.

The psychological impact on Bob Holleman worsened after Christi's body was found. He went to the medical examiner's office to see the body and later told Molly that at first he, too, thought the remains were those of a little boy. Except for one thing: the single Cabbage Patch Shoe the dead child was wearing. He came home and broke down when he saw his wife. "They couldn't even tell what she was," he sobbed.

Yet, instead of taking some solace in the fact that at least the question of what happened to Christi was answered and her remains returned to her family, Holleman's depression deepened. Molly worried. She never once asked him to stop or give it up—she was proud of the sort of detective he was—but she knew it wasn't healthy; not for him, nor their family.

She was slammed by that fact one day when she came home from work. She saw his car in the driveway and knew he was home, but she couldn't find him, and he wouldn't answer her calls. The last place she looked was the closet in their bedroom, and there was her strong, smart, funny police officer husband curled up on the floor, crying in the dark with a gun in his hand.

CHAPTER TWO

February 12, 1986

The darkness sat in the driver's seat of his white van waiting patiently as the little girl walked towards him on her way to the nearby elementary school. Like any predator, he'd scouted the lay of the land, checked for hidden dangers—such as police cars and potential witnesses—sized up the pretty, brown-eyed, dark-haired child, and now he waited for her to move to within striking distance.

Metaphorically, as a predator he was no lion willing to take on prey larger than himself or capable of harming him in the process. A base coward, he relied on stealth and cunning to surprise and ambush victims much smaller than himself and unable to put up any sort of defense. He was persistent; if he missed, or his intended victim got away, he kept hunting until he succeeded.

With pale blue eyes, a thick but neatly trimmed moustache, and brown hair with long bangs swept left to right, he didn't look like a monster. His most distinguishing feature was a large mole above his right eyebrow; otherwise he was just an unexceptional-looking, young white man of average height and weight. But beneath the exterior he was much more than that.

For years, he'd stalked elementary schools, neighborhoods, and playgrounds looking for young girls to abduct, rape, and murder. With some exceptions, he concentrated on black, Asian, or Hispanic girls living in low-income areas. He thought of them as "throwaway kids"—hardly missed and soon forgotten, except by those who loved them; just sad cold case files gathering dust in police records rooms.

As though invisible, he brazenly struck in broad daylight, pulling children into his van or cars, or he crept into homes in the dead of night to carry away little girls while their families slept. He was every parent's worst nightmare: the bogeyman they warned their children about, disguised as the friendly stranger who offered candy, cookies, and ice cream to entice his victims close enough to grab; the fiend who lurked in the shadows outside of bedroom windows.

Then, when he was finished with his atrocities, he'd dump the tiny bodies in remote areas, crossing jurisdictional lines in order to confuse the efforts of law enforcement agencies. Weeks, months, even years passed before someone would find the remains … if they were found … during which time the grieving families wondered what had become of their little girls. And even if their horrific fates became known, time passed agonizingly slow with no answer to the question of who could have done such vicious things to a child.

The bogeyman hunted with impunity while authorities scattered across multiple states weren't even aware that a single killer was responsible for so many child-abduction murders. It gave him a sense of invincibility. He believed that he was smarter than the police, that they'd never catch him. And so far, he was right. Hell, he'd had that little blonde, Christi Meeks, in the trunk of his car when that Mesquite police officer pulled him over on the way out of town. But he'd talked his way out of it and was soon on his way to Lake

Texoma to enjoy his prize.

On this day, he was parked on Waterfall Lane in a lower-income, working-class neighborhood in North Dallas, Texas, near Dobie Elementary School when he spotted ten-year-old Tiffany Ibarra. With her dark hair and olive complexion—her father was Hispanic and her mother Caucasian—she fit the physical profile of his preferred victims.

However, Tiffany's appearance wasn't all that put her in danger. Far more perilous was that she was alone, though that was not by choice or her parents' lack of oversight. Normally, she would have walked to school with several friends. However, a bird had defecated on her clothes that morning, so she'd returned home to change and then had to walk back to school by herself.

Now, as the little girl approached the van, the killer climbed out and moved towards her. Although he was smiling, something about him warned her to run. She bolted, but it was too late. He caught her within ten feet, grabbing her by her backpack. He then wrapped his arms around the struggling child and carried her back to the van. Opening the side door and pushing her in, he climbed up behind her.

The killer planned to take Tiffany to a secluded wooded area in the country he'd already picked out. There, he could sexually assault the terrified little girl at his leisure before choking the life out of her. Then he'd throw her away like so much garbage and be on his way, satiated for the moment, laughing to himself about how he'd once again struck while the stupid police were helpless to prevent him from hunting wherever and whenever he wanted.

However, on this day something was different. The killer stared at Tiffany for several minutes before asking her for her home telephone number. When she told him, he called the number on an early version of a cellular telephone known as a "bag phone," a new technological marvel in 1986, and then handed it to her.

"Tell your mother you've been kidnapped," he demanded.

Tiffany did as told when her mother answered. But before she could say anything else, the killer grabbed the phone back and hung up.

"You better not walk to school alone again," he warned the girl. "I've been watching you, and the next time I won't let you go." He then opened the door of the van and told her to get out.

Tiffany ran home terrified and in tears. The killer followed in his van until she reached the driveway of the apartment complex where she lived. He then sped away.

When her daughter burst through the front door screaming, Theresa Ibarra was getting dressed to go out and look for her. She thought Tiffany had made up the story she told her on the telephone as an excuse to get out of going to class and was more angry than worried. However, the girl insisted that she was now telling the truth so they drove through the neighborhood looking for a white van. When the search proved fruitless, they went to the school, where Theresa had her daughter tell her story to the principal, who then called the Dallas Police Department.

The officers arrived and took statements from Tiffany and her mother. But with nothing else to go on, they returned to their other duties. Who knew if the little girl was telling the truth or wanted to skip school, as her mother thought possible? No one else had reported a suspicious white van and a man stalking children. And why make the effort to grab her from a sidewalk just to warn her and then let her go?

Tragically, Tiffany wasn't a liar. Three days later, on February 15, the day after Valentine's Day, Christie Proctor was walking home from a friend's house on Waterfall Lane when the bogeyman struck again. No one saw him take the little dark-haired girl who was just a few days shy of her tenth birthday and dressed in a pink-and-white sweater, blue jeans, and old white tennis shoes. The only clue left behind to indicate that she had passed that way was a crushed heart-shaped plastic box given to her by her aunt for Valentine's Day. Searching for her daughter, Laura Proctor saw it lying on the ground and knew that was where her daughter had been taken. She'd felt in that moment, the terror her daughter had experienced.

However, there was only one witness. A resident of the neighborhood, Alberta Abundis, told police that she noticed a strange man driving a white van with brown stripes slowly through the neighborhood. She'd got a pretty good look at him, too—a white man with a large mole on the right side of his face.

The Dallas Police Department investigators realized that a predator was hunting the area around Dobie Elementary. They returned to the Ibarra house and this time interviewed Tiffany more thoroughly. A police artist created a sketch from her description of her kidnapper, an ordinary-looking, young white man with dark hair parted in the middle, and a thick, neat moustache.

Now the police knew Tiffany was telling the truth; only it was too late. This time, the bogeyman did not release the pretty little maiden.

CHAPTER THREE

October 5, 1986

Dorothy Sherrill stepped outside her home in tiny Thorntown, Indiana, to call her children in for lunch. It was an unseasonably warm and sunny afternoon for that time of year, and the children in the small trailer court they lived in were making the most of it, playing hide-and-seek.

Six-year-old Shannon and two-year-old David had spent the weekend with Dorothy's estranged husband, but now they were back home. She immediately spotted David in the front yard and some of the other children running through the neighborhood. But she didn't see her daughter.

"Where's Shannon?" she asked her son.

"Sissy went behind the trailer."

Dorothy walked over to where her son pointed, but Shannon wasn't there. Twenty more minutes of calling for her and hunting around the neighborhood also came up empty. Shannon's playmates didn't know where she'd gone. And although many people were out working in their yards and enjoying the pleasant Sunday afternoon, no one had seen the little barefoot girl in the white sundress with blue trim.

Starting to panic, Dorothy contacted the town marshal, Gary L. Campbell, who responded at 1:53 p.m. and talked to some of the other children and neighbors.

He figured she'd just wandered off and surely someone would have seen her. But when that line of questioning didn't result in any answers, he really began to worry and knew he needed help. Campbell only had one other officer working for him in Thorntown, a small, farming community forty miles northwest of Indianapolis with a population at the time of maybe fifteen hundred, so he called for assistance.

Typical of a small, rural county, the various police agencies in Boone County, where Thorntown was located, often covered for each other, monitoring each other's radio calls and responding with assistance. And that's what happened when the call for help went out: The Indiana State Patrol and Boone County Sheriff's Office soon had officers at the scene. By 2:30, members of the volunteer fire department, the various law enforcement agencies, and a volunteer group of more than one hundred and fifty citizens began combing the area.

They checked wooded areas and creek beds, inside sheds, and under porches, and went door to door, asking if anyone had seen Shannon. One volunteer even flew his private plane over the town and surroundings. But the sun set, and still there was no sign of her.

The ground search continued throughout the night, and the next morning the hunt for Shannon ramped up. Helicopters flew over the area, and lawmen from more outside agencies, including the FBI and the Indianapolis Police Department, arrived to help. Children on bicycles distributed copies of her photograph from house to house.

Bloodhounds were brought in, and they quickly hit on a scent trail that led searchers to a field where they found what they believed to be her footprints. The prints headed towards the town cemetery. Two more sets of tracks belonging to men were also located near the child's prints, but there was no telling if they were all connected, and they all ended in the cemetery.

As the day passed with still no sign of Shannon, there was a growing sense of helplessness among the law enforcement officers and the community. They'd done everything they knew how to do and come up empty. It was clear that Shannon had not just wandered off—someone had taken her, and they all knew that the more time that passed, the less chance they had of finding her unharmed and alive.

Fear gripped the townspeople. A monster who took children from their yards in the middle of the afternoon was loose, and everybody was on edge. This sort of thing didn't happen in Thorntown. It wasn't the big city with those kinds of crimes; the entire county only had a population of 35,000. Fear fueled anger and paranoia. There were instances in which volunteers going house to house attempted to break into residences when the inhabitants were slow to answer the doorbell.

As night fell on the second day of Shannon's abduction, the ground search was called off. No amount of shouting her name or hoping for the sight of her was going to locate the little girl; she was gone.

In the days that followed, the investigation changed from searching for Shannon to looking for a suspect. The children who were playing with Shannon were also hypnotized to see if they'd remember anything or anyone, but there was nothing of any substance. Detectives questioned Dorothy and Mike Sherrill. It wouldn't have been the first time that a child had disappeared during a divorce, even if, as in their case, there was no animosity between the parents or a custody dispute. They then took lie detector tests and passed.

There was just so little for investigators to work with. It was hard to believe that no one in the neighborhood of the trailer court had seen anything. People were out taking care of their lawns, or working on their cars; one guy was roofing. Yet, there were only three reports of anything even remotely unusual. One man said he glimpsed a little girl riding in a red pickup truck. Two other people reported seeing a white van they didn't recognize driving slowly through the neighborhood.

But even if the truck or the van was the suspect's vehicle, where had he gone? Thorntown was just a few miles from Interstate 65, which ran a hundred and fifty miles north to Chicago, and forty miles the other direction to Indianapolis, and then on to Louisville, Kentucky and other points south. Or Shannon's abductor could have turned onto Interstate 70 in Indianapolis and headed to Ohio towards Columbus, two hundred miles east, or west to St. Louis.

In the time it took between Dorothy Sherrill noticing that Shannon was gone and contacting the town marshal and the additional half hour it took for other officers to respond, the bogeyman could have driven a hundred miles. Or he might have simply taken Shannon to any one of a number of isolated parks and woodlands in that rural part of western Indiana before disappearing down the web of interconnected highways and interstates.

No one realized it at the time, but the disappearance of Shannon Sherrill would haunt the community of Thorntown, including the police officers who investigated the case, long after her friends had grown up, graduated high school, married, had children of their own.

One of those officers was a young Indiana State

trooper named Jeff Heck, who'd been home with his wife and two-year-old son in Lebanon, the Boone County seat, when he got called in to help. As a uniformed trooper, Heck's responsibilities consisted of searching the area, doing neighborhood checks, and interviewing possible witnesses.

When he returned home that night, Heck drew his family close. His wife was a school teacher, and with their occupations and the sometimes dark ways of the world, over the years there would be many instances when they would feel the need to hug their children a little tighter. This was one of those times, albeit without knowing that someday, many years in the future, he would again be asked to help find the man who took Shannon Sherrill.

CHAPTER FOUR

November 3, 1987

As he drove down the alley away from the elementary school where he'd been lurking, the killer spotted the two little girls picking wildflowers in the field across from a large apartment complex. The younger child was hardly more than a toddler—petite, pretty, black-haired, and doe-eyed. But he had his eye on the other girl who also looked Hispanic and appeared to be about five years old.

He pulled his gray sedan over to the curb near them. Getting out of the car, he called out. "I have some candy for you," he said with a smile.

The older girl, Julia Diaz, looked at the young white man as he approached and shook her head. "He's lying," she said to her little friend, Roxann Reyes. She then screamed and dodged as the man lunged for her.

The killer chased Julia across the street, but she slipped through a narrow opening between two of the apartment buildings where he couldn't follow. Snarling, he ran around the building, hoping to intercept her on the other side. Instead, he nearly bumped into an older woman named Wanda Huggins. For a moment they locked eyes then he turned and ran back to his car where he discovered the younger child was still standing next to his vehicle.

Just three years old, Roxann didn't know what to

make of her friend's reaction or the stranger who'd offered candy. Trusting, innocent she waited in her light pink shorts and purple top and didn't attempt to flee when the man returned. Her world changed, however, when he punched her hard in the stomach and, as the terrified child gasped for air, threw her in the car. A moment later, he was in the driver's seat and speeding from the neighborhood.

Meanwhile, having narrowly escaped the stranger, Julia Diaz ran in terror for the apartment manager's office on the far end of the complex. Roxann's mother, Tammy, was the manager and Julia thought she'd find her there.

However, Julia actually ran past where Roxann's mother and father, Sergio Reyes, were working to get an apartment ready to rent. Tammy was inside the apartment cleaning and making small repairs. Sergio was out in front cutting carpet to replace the old, worn-out remnants. Each believing that their daughter was with the other, neither parent knew that Roxann had wandered across the street to pick wildflowers with her friend Julia.

The first clue that something was wrong wasn't even perceived as a threat. Sergio heard a car door slam and a vehicle race off on the other side of the building from where he was working, but that wasn't uncommon. Nor did he notice Julia Diaz squeeze out from an opening between the buildings and race for the manager's office.

By the time Julia found someone to tell about the strange man who chased her, and for concerned adults to then tell Roxann's parents, it was too late. The bogeyman and his three-year-old victim were gone.

In Ohio, Joyce Davis had just returned from visiting one of her daughters near her home in Minford when a neighbor hurried up to her. "Something's happened in Texas," the woman said. "Tammy wants you to call."

Davis hurried into her home to call her daughter. Tammy was her first born of nine children—eight girls and one boy. Only fifteen when she delivered Tammy, Davis married Tammy's father, and together they'd conceived the rest of the kids over a twelve-year span. It was a lot of children for a young mother, but the rural acreage where they were raised provided plenty of room, and the girls grew up as rough-and-tumble as their brother.

Headstrong and tough, Tammy was also married and pregnant in her teens. She bore two daughters, but she wasn't ready to take care of kids on her own, so Joyce raised them.

After divorcing her first husband and looking for a fresh start, Tammy left Ohio with a girlfriend and moved to Texas. There, she met and married Sergio Reyes. Their little girl, Roxann, was born in January 1984. This time, Tammy, who felt that she'd "missed out" on her first two daughters, wasn't giving up her child. In fact, after she got settled in Texas, she even thought about sending for the other two but realized that they'd grown up counting on Joyce; and it would break their hearts, and her mother's, to split them up now. So she left them in Ohio and compensated with the affection she and her husband showered on Roxann.

Unlike her country-girl mother, Roxann was a little princess who liked dresses and all the traditionally "girlie" things. She was petite, even for her age, and smart; somehow both spoiled rotten and well-mannered.

The family didn't have much money. Tammy worked as the manager of the low-rent apartment complex in Garland, and Sergio helped as the maintenance man, as well as working odd jobs. The run-down neighborhood was known for its drug dealing, prostitution, and criminal element, but Tammy was a hard worker, and she had plans to better her life and that of her family.

Those plans disappeared in the first waves of terror after she was told that Roxann was missing. When her mother called, she sobbed. "Mom, Roxann's missing. Some man took her."

Joyce told her daughter that she'd be there as quickly as possible. She then hung up and called her mother in Cincinnati and told her what had happened. Twelve hours later, they were in Garland, Texas; other than for gas and to run to the service station restroom, they had not stopped nor had anything to eat or drink.

When they pulled up to the apartment complex, Joyce's mom broke down and wouldn't get out of the car. Nor would she leave the vehicle for the next three days as she holed up, watching the entrance to the complex for Roxann to come home.

Joyce felt as if she were living a nightmare, unable to wake up or do much to comfort her crumbling daughter. Along with other family members, who had driven to Garland, and Tammy's neighbors, they searched everywhere, every culvert, every field. They distributed flyers with the police artist's sketch of the suspect as he'd been described by Julia Diaz: a young, white man with the brown moustache, dark hair with long bangs swept to the side, and a large mole on the right side of his face above the eyebrow.

Tammy beat herself up. "I should have never let her go out and play," she cried over and over to her mother. "I should have watched her more carefully." And in the cruel way of such tragedies, she and Sergio looked at each other with accusations in their eyes.

Other people said cruel things, too, or gave sideways glances that said more than words ever could have: they'd failed to protect their daughter; they weren't fit parents. But the cruelest were the prank callers who pretended to be kidnappers.

As the FBI listened in, the first of those told Tammy to put ten thousand dollars in an envelope and deliver it where they said. "Or we'll cut off her ear."

Another caller went so far as to demand a ransom and arrange for the drop-off at the airport. As she'd been coaxed by the federal agents, Tammy asked, "How do we know you have her?"

"We'll send you her finger in the mail!"

Tammy screamed and dissolved into hysterical tears. But there was hope. If Roxann had been kidnapped for a ransom then, perhaps, they'd still get her back.

On the morning of the drop-off, the FBI and local law enforcement officers sealed off the airport and flooded it with their own agents and officers. But the kidnapper never showed up, nor did some grisly token arrive in the mail.

Roxann's kidnapper didn't want money. He wanted something far more precious and didn't care about the damage done when he cast this stone into a dark pond of nightmares without end.

PART II

A Case of Divine Intervention

CHAPTER FIVE

June 1996

Gary Sweet opened the door of the "murder closet" and stepped inside. The small, windowless room in the basement of the Garland Police Department held the agency's files for unsolved murders stacked in row after row, from floor to ceiling, in bankers' boxes. Contained within each were the ghosts of justice interrupted, of nightmares without end, and of tears uncounted. Waiting for someone to care.

The thirty-seven-year-old detective was on his lunch hour and had decided to spend it looking through the old files, mostly out of curiosity. It wasn't as if he had nothing else to do. A satellite of Dallas, Garland was actually the tenth largest city in Texas, bigger than Amarillo. Working in the crimes against persons unit, which included felonies from harassment to murder, his caseload averaged sixty-five to seventy cases a month. Killers, thugs, robbers, and rapists did not take holidays so that he would have time to solve old homicide cases.

Still, he was relatively new to detective work after serving nine years as a late-night patrolman and another two as a school resource officer, and cold cases fascinated him. Part of it was the challenge of putting the pieces together to find, arrest, and convict killers when the original investigators had failed. But more importantly, it troubled him that killers were living out their lives thinking they'd gotten away with murder while the families of the victims suffered without resolution.

Tall and athletic with a soft Texas drawl, Sweet never intended to be a police officer, much less a detective. He was the son of a stay-at-home mom and a milk deliveryman who had worked for the same dairy for forty years. With two older sisters and one younger brother, his childhood was normal for a boy raised in a working-class neighborhood of Dallas; nothing in his upbringing would have predicted a future in law enforcement. He'd been very involved in high school sports, particularly football and basketball, and in martial arts. In fact, he'd once dreamed of being the world heavyweight champion in kickboxing, but that dream derailed at age 19 when he married his high school sweetheart, Julie Miller. He fought his last tournament two weeks following his wedding, but then the exigency of taking care of his wife and, two years after the wedding, their first daughter meant an end to his aspirations as a professional fighter.

So Sweet got a job unloading railroad cars. It paid well and he had no other plans, but that changed in 1983 when he was laid off.

Initially, he applied to join the Garland Police Department only to qualify for an unemployment check. However, his best friend was a cop and invited him to ride along on his patrol one evening, which was enough to at least interest him in the possibility of becoming an officer. So he signed up for the entrance exam.

When he arrived to take the test and discovered there were three hundred other applicants for fifteen positions, he almost turned around and left. But he had nothing else to do, plus a wife and child to take care of, so he stayed and passed the written test, as well as the physical agility test the next day. Even then, it was several months before he learned he'd been accepted to the police academy, which he had to graduate from to work for the Garland Police Department.

Sweet excelled at the academy, was hired by the Garland PD, and two years after starting as a night patrolman who loved the "late night action," he was teaching self-defense courses to other officers. However, it was more than a paycheck and more than the adrenaline of battling criminals that convinced him he was meant to be a cop.

In 1978, he'd become a Christian and started praying for guidance on what to do with his life. As he'd passed each test and then was accepted into the academy and finally hired, he'd come to believe that God's plan was for him to work in law enforcement. He even applied his faith to his work. He'd discovered soon after starting as a police officer that he had a gift for talking to people and a knack for getting criminals to trust him and even break down and confess their crimes. Those who protested their innocence by saying how godly they were would get a dose of Biblical verse from him, particularly Proverbs 28:13: *"Whoever conceals their sins does not prosper, but the one who confesses and renounces them, finds mercy."* And it often worked.

When his former employer called and asked him to return to the rail yard, he declined, though it meant living with the large pay cut to continue on his road to a career in law enforcement. He'd never regretted the decision and believed he'd been given a sign that his path was preordained when his former employer subsequently went out of business.

Although he'd surprised her when he said he was going to try to get onto the Garland police force, Julie supported his decision. She wasn't worried even after she attended a seminar at the academy for wives and girlfriends of the cadets in which they were told what to expect—the long hours, the dangers, the emotional toll of dealing with all the misery and suffering created by criminals, even other women who were attracted to police officers, married or not. The divorce rate for police officers, they were warned, was horrendous. However, Julie didn't worry about her husband's faithfulness or his ability to deal with the pressures of the job. She was proud of him and knew he loved his work.

In fact, if there was one thing that bothered him, it was when there was no action. He wanted to protect people and "save the world," and he'd get antsy if at any particular moment it didn't need saving.

Thirteen years after he got his first paycheck as a police officer, he entered the "murder closet." Later he would come to believe that divine providence had moved him that day when alone in that small, sad room, Sweet began looking through the file boxes. He found one in which three young black children had been found dead in an abandoned freezer. The original investigator concluded that they'd crawled in and were accidentally trapped. But looking at the photographs of their bodies—packed into the small space like sardines—Sweet thought there was no way they got in by themselves. Someone just hadn't cared enough about those children to look any further.

He was still thinking about that case when he noticed a box labeled with a name he recognized: Roxann Reyes. Even before he opened it, he was aware of some of what it would contain. He'd been working the late shift as a patrol officer in the same area of Garland where she'd last been seen and was briefed about the case before he went out on patrol that night. He knew that Roxann was a three-year-old girl who'd been abducted and murdered in November 1987. With two little girls of his own, the crime had struck him harder than many others and still weighed on his heart now as he opened the box and pulled out the first file.

The exact elements of the case had blurred in the time since he first heard about the child's disappearance. But now as he read, they returned in vivid detail. Roxann had been picking wildflowers one afternoon with her friend, six-year-old Julia Diaz, when a man approached them on a street behind the low-rent, crime-ridden apartment complex Roxanne's mother, Tammy, managed. The monster took Roxann fifteen miles to a remote location near the small town of Murphy, Texas, where he raped and strangled her. He then dumped her body in the woods where her remains were found a year later.

At the time it occurred, Roxann's abduction had reminded Sweet of a similar case two years earlier: the January 1985 disappearance of five-year-old Christi Meeks, who disappeared in Mesquite, Texas while playing hide-and-seek outside of an apartment complex, and the February 1986 abduction of Christie Proctor whose body had been found in a field beneath an old, burned mattress near Plano, Texas.

Sweet and his young family had been living in Mesquite at the time of Meeks' kidnapping, and like any parent, especially one with young daughters, the case had resonated with him. After Roxann was abducted, he'd wondered if the three cases were connected, but he'd never heard anything more about them.

Nine years had now passed since Roxann's murder. Sweet's three daughters were sixteen, eleven, and three, happy and safe, a joy to him and his wife. Picking up and reading the Reyes case report, he recalled how sorry he'd felt for Roxann, whose fate it had been to be raised in a neighborhood rife with drug dealers and prostitutes, and then murdered by a cold-blooded monster. But he also couldn't imagine the devastation heaped upon the girl's mother and father, Tammy and Sergio Reyes, or their lingering sorrow, exacerbated by the lack of resolution. It troubled him that justice for Roxann and her parents moldered in the murder closet of the Garland Police Department.

Glancing through the Reyes case evidence, Sweet was appalled to find that it was mostly an unorganized collection of papers, photographs, notepads, and sticky notes with undecipherable messages on them, newspaper clippings, and a few recordings. It would take more time to make sense of it than he had during his lunch hour, but one folder caught his eye; it contained records pertaining to a long list of possible suspects.

Some of the records had little more than a name and a few notes in them. Others had a bit more, and one of those was labeled "David Elliot Penton." Sweet read that in April 1991 Penton was convicted in Columbus, Ohio, for the murder of Nydra Ross, a nine-year-old black girl, who'd disappeared in March 1988 and whose remains were discovered in September of that year in a heavily wooded creek bed. According to a Columbus newspaper story in the file, Penton, then thirty-two years old, was a fugitive from Texas, where he'd been convicted in 1985 of involuntary manslaughter after shaking his own infant son to death in Fort Hood. He'd been sentenced to five years but had been released on a bond pending appeal and subsequently fled the state. Nydra had been murdered by Penton while he was a fugitive.

What got Sweet's attention was that Roxann's mother, Tammy Reyes, was also from Ohio and that her parents, Joyce and Paul Davis, lived in Minford, near Columbus. Apparently, Paul had seen the newspaper article about the Ross case and noticed that Penton's mug shot closely resembled the composite police sketch from Julia Diaz's description of the man who'd abducted Roxann and that he was a fugitive from Texas. Davis had driven to the Columbus Police Department and told them about his granddaughter's murder in Texas.

Sweet saw that at some point in time—it was difficult to tell exactly when from the disorganized file—the Columbus investigators called the Garland Police Department. But there was nothing more in the file to indicate what, if anything had come of that call. In fact, he couldn't tell from the file if Penton remained a viable suspect in the Texas murders or had been cleared. Except for the connection to the Columbus murder case and the suspicions raised by Roxann's grandparents, he was just one of maybe a hundred names in the suspect folder.

The Reyes case intrigued Sweet, but there were six other detectives and a supervisor in his unit, all of who had more experience than he did. Even if he'd wanted to work a cold case, he didn't think he'd be allowed to or was qualified. So he closed the box on Roxann Reyes and left the murder closet to return to his regular caseload. Justice for the little girl and her family would have to wait.

CHAPTER SIX

July 1998

As the next two years passed, Sweet's thoughts often turned to Roxann Reyes. Sometimes other crimes against children would bring her to mind. But it wasn't always something specific. A name or image from the files would come to him out of the blue, as if he was being reminded not to forget that the little girl and her family were waiting. Other cases would come and go, but Roxann's unsolved murder hovered on the edge of his consciousness like a bad dream.

However, the time wasn't wasted. He didn't know it yet, but every day he spent as a detective, each case he solved, every criminal he caught, was preparing him for the day when he would begin to pursue Roxann's killer.

As a detective in the Garland PD Crimes Against Persons Bureau, his caseload involved a wide spectrum of violent offenses. But of those, murder—the taking of a life—was the ultimate crime, the one that could not be undone or from which the victim could not recover. Yet, even homicides came in shades of gray.

He hated to think of any murder as "routine," but some were just plain darker than others and would have greater impact on him as a man and as a detective. One of those was the murder of Smiley Johnson, an 80-year-old woman, who was viciously attacked in 1996 shortly after he looked at the Roxann Reyes case files.

The old woman was assaulted in the early morning hours in the bedroom of her house, where she been slashed and stabbed eighteen times in her torso. The onslaught was brutal; blood was everywhere, soaking into the red shag carpet of the room. Her stomach had been sliced open so that her intestines protruded. But Johnson hadn't died right away.

After her assailant left, she'd staggered out to her living room and called a neighbor, who lived across the street. The woman hurried over and found her friend collapsed in a growing pool of blood but still conscious. It was the neighbor who then dialed 911.

When the dispatcher learned that the victim was still alive, she asked to speak to Smiley Johnson. "Do you know who attacked you?"

"He came to the back door," Smiley replied. "I thought it was my nephew, so I let him in." But then she said she wasn't so sure that it was her nephew; all she knew was that the intruder was a small, white male.

The tough, old woman was taken to the hospital by helicopter, but not in time to save her life. Assigned to the homicide case, Sweet and his partner, John McDonald, didn't have much to go on, except the general description of the killer. They started by trying to find out everything they could about the victim by talking to her family.

The detectives learned that Smiley had a daughter, who was in prison on drug and forgery charges; and that the old woman had pretty much raised her daughter's two boys, both of who were also well-known to the Garland Police Department, though mostly for petty crimes. The victim doted on her grandsons and didn't think much of the police, especially when it came to protecting her family from them. One of the older Garland detectives told Sweet that he'd gone over to her house once to arrest one of the grandsons and the tiny old woman had planted herself between the detective and her boy; so he'd had to arrest her *and* the young man. Even if one of the grandsons was her killer, the detective warned Sweet, she would have lied to protect him.

Apparently, the grandsons felt the same about her and were devastated by her murder. Or so they said, but they still needed to be cleared. In fact, one of the grandsons was small-statured and had immediately become a potential suspect. Sweet flew to Atlanta, where the man lived, and questioned him, but he had an alibi that crossed him off the list.

The other grandson lived in Florida. He seemed particularly upset over her death and often called Sweet to check on the investigation's progress. He had given the two detectives an important clue early in the investigation when he told Sweet that his grandmother owned a big, mean dog who wouldn't have allowed just anybody to come in through the back door. If the killer was a stranger, the dog would have "chewed his ass up," the grandson assured Sweet.

The presence of a protective dog indicated that the killer was likely to be a member of the family or someone else well-known to the animal. So based on what the grandsons said, as well as what Johnson told the 911 operator, the detectives interviewed several of the woman's nephews; but they were all decent, law-abiding men, and all of them had alibis. The partners even interviewed two great-grandsons, 17 and 15 years old; Sweet talked to the older one and McDonald to the younger, but neither seemed to be a likely suspect.

Making the lack of progress more frustrating, the detectives believed that Smiley Johnson wasn't the killer's only victim. A week after Johnson's murder, a young black woman was also attacked during the early morning hours in her home just a few blocks from Johnson's house. The assailant stabbed her more than a dozen times, but she'd survived. The timing, location, and nature of the attack, which could only be described as a frenzied bloodbath, suggested a connection to Johnson's murder. However, the victim in the second case described her attacker as an older black man.

The scenario of two different assailants committing such a similar crime, in such a similar way, in the same general neighborhood, didn't add up for Sweet and McDonald. What made sense was that there was a single killer on the loose. What's more, a bloodhound brought in to track the black woman's assailant followed him back to Johnson's house, but there the trail grew cold. So did the case.

Then about a year after Johnson's murder, Sweet got a telephone call from the great-grandson he'd interviewed. He said his younger cousin, Michael Giles, the then-15-year-old whom McDonald had questioned, had just told him that he'd murdered their great-grandmother; in fact, he said, Michael seemed proud of it.

The next day and at Sweet's urging, the older cousin agreed to wear a wire and speak to the younger boy and get him to talk about the murder again. As Sweet listened in on the conversation, Michael Giles not only admitted attacking his great-grandmother, he bragged about stabbing the young black woman as well.

When Sweet arrested the young man, Michael was living in Johnson's house and sleeping in the bedroom where she'd been attacked. It was the first clue that his interrogation of the teen at the Garland police station was going to be bizarre.

Sweet had to work the case on his own; after the original interviews with the teens, McDonald had been killed in a plane crash. So he sat the teen down in a sparsely furnished interview room containing within its stark white walls two chairs on opposite sides of a steel table. Taking a seat across from Giles, he studied the short, slight teenager, who favored the "Goth" look, with stringy, dyed-black hair and pale skin. He confronted him, flat-out accusing Giles of being the killer.

To Sweet's surprise, Giles didn't try to deny it. In fact, he shrugged and calmly began talking about his despicable acts like someone else might describe a day at the beach. Although revolted, Sweet went with it and let Giles prattle on. Except for the topic, they could have been two guys discussing a ball game over a beer; as he warmed up to the detective, the teenager spoke and acted like they were old friends and that Sweet was someone who really understood him. He seemed to enjoy recalling the lurid details.

Sweet knew from studying the case files that everything Giles said was corroborated by the evidence. For instance, during the initial investigation, crime scene technicians used luminol, a chemical that reacts with iron in blood, to be able to see bloodstains in the red carpeting. They could clearly follow the bloody footprints of the killer as he went from the bedroom to the bathroom, where he washed his hands, and then out the back door. All of that matched Giles' description of his actions, as he recalled them step-by-step for Sweet.

Giles also explained why the bloodhound had followed his trail from the young, black woman's home to his great-grandmother's after the second attack. He said that even before he started living in the house, he liked to go back and climb up on the roof, where he would sit in the moonlight and relive the murder in his mind. Then after attacking the young woman, he'd returned to Johnson's roof and fantasized about his acts.

Throughout the interview, Giles broke into chants praising Satan, and he kept mentioning a specific time, "2:13," which Sweet found odd. But of all the twisted, demented things the killer said, one of the oddest was that he had loved his great-grandmother.

"Then why did you do it?" Sweet asked.

Giles shrugged. "I wanted to know what it was like to have sex with a dead person."

Sweet scowled. He was so familiar with the evidence in the case that he'd known every detail before Giles described them. So he was aware that Smiley had been tested for sexual assault during her autopsy and that the results were negative. "Now I know you're lying to me, Michael," he said.

For the first time, Giles' face flushed in anger. "I damn sure did," he snarled. "I raped her through one of her stab wounds. I even licked her intestines that were sticking out!"

Nauseated but trying not to react, Sweet was sure at that moment that he was in the presence of true evil; not just a killer, but some wicked monster that prowled beyond the circle of humanity. Giles had no remorse for his actions. He'd wanted to know what it was like to have sex with a dead body, so he'd attacked his great-grandmother, a woman he professed to love. Then he'd stabbed the young black woman for no particular reason, other than a lust for blood, the pleasure of inflicting pain, and the deviant sexual gratification he derived from it.

Sweet was disgusted, listening to the vicious, evil creature that was Michael Giles, as the teen willingly and with a great deal of satisfaction recounted the horrors he'd inflicted on other human beings. But the detective needed to know as much about the suspect as he could, so he controlled his anger and revulsion and acted as if the vile admissions were the sorts of trivial events he heard every day as a law officer.

Even after the confession, Sweet continued trying to understand what made Giles tick. The teen's mother supplied some of that, even though, as she told the detective, she still loved her son. She brought Sweet her boy's music collection, most of it from two bands: *Cannibal Corpse*, a "death metal band" self-described as "the reigning kings of brutality;" and *Slayer*, a "thrash metal" band.

Sweet brought the recordings home to see if there was anything in the music that would give him some insight into Giles. Just one look at the CD covers and his wife wouldn't let him bring them into the house. He understood her feelings, especially after he'd already played the audiotape of his interview with Giles for her. She didn't want any more of Giles' evil invading her home.

Returning the CD's to the office, Sweet began studying them to see if there was anything that would explain Giles' behavior. He was looking at the song list on one *Slayer* CD, when he noticed a song called "2:13." He'd suspected at the time of the first interview that Giles was quoting from a song; now he knew which one.

Sweet looked up the lyrics for the song on the internet and discovered that "2:13" was a song about necrophilia.

> *"Erotic sensations tingle my spine*
> *A dead body lying next to mine*

Smooth blue black lips
I start salivating as we kiss."

Sweet had no idea this was the sort of "music" teens were listening to. He got off the internet, sickened by the thought that music might influence an evil person such as Michael Giles to act out his fantasies.

Inwardly, the detective could not begin to fathom the workings of Giles' disturbed mind. But it was also hard to understand why Smiley Johnson, who had to have known it was her great-grandson who had done such vile things to her, protected him. Making matters worse, her silence had resulted in at least one more victim, the young black woman.

Then again, the second victim wasn't a lot of help either. After Giles' confession, Sweet went to talk to her and ask if she was sure about her description of her assailant. She was adamant; her attacker was an older black man.

It didn't make sense. Sweet then asked her if she actually saw her attacker's face. No, she hadn't. He asked if she'd looked at his hands and that's how she knew he was a black man. No, she didn't. Did he say something that gave away his race? No, he never spoke the entire time he was stabbing her over and over again.

Shaking his head in confusion, Sweet asked her on what evidence she'd based her conclusion that her attacker was an older black man. She told him it was because of the neighborhood she lived in, which was 80 percent black. In other words, she was playing the odds. "So what makes you think he was older?" he asked.

"Because I saw his shoes," the woman replied defiantly. "He was wearing black, high-top canvas basketball shoes. No kid would wear shoes like that."

Sweet was dumbfounded. He knew what kind of

shoes she was talking about: "Chuck Taylor" Converse All-Stars; he'd worn them in high school himself. But more importantly, the familiar tread design had been found in the blood on the floor at both crime scenes, and they were the type of shoes Michael Giles was wearing when Sweet arrested him. Yet, when Sweet told the woman that they'd arrested a young white male wearing those shoes for a murder two blocks away, she still maintained that her original description was correct.

Michael Giles was charged for the murder of his great-grandmother, but because of the second victim's obstinacy, he was not also charged with attempted murder. Sweet was disappointed he couldn't make the second case, if only for insurance purposes. If Giles had been an adult, he might have faced the death penalty, but because of his age, he could only get prison time. Adding a second attempted murder charge would have meant more time in prison.

Sweet worried about what would happen if Giles was ever released. He was convinced that the teenager was a serial killer in the making. He'd only been successful once, but he tried a second time. It was obvious he enjoyed killing and felt no remorse; if he got the chance, Sweet was convinced, Giles would kill again.

As the day of the trial approached, Sweet wondered how a jury would react to the shocking details of Giles' confession and his obsession with necrophilia. However, no jury ever heard the case. Instead of going to trial, Giles agreed at the last minute to plead guilty in exchange for a thirty-year sentence.

Not nearly enough time, Sweet thought, and Giles would still be young enough when he got out to commit more murders. But the judge had only seen a frightened, small-statured, sixteen-year-old boy in front of him at sentencing, not the malevolent killer Sweet knew was lurking beneath the surface. The judge sent Giles to a juvenile facility until age 18, at which point he would be moved to an adult prison to wait for his first parole board in 2014.

Sweet walked away from the case having learned valuable lessons and with greater understanding of his role as a guardian who stood between evil and good, and the burden that placed on him. He knew that he couldn't really talk about some aspects of the job with anyone but another cop, not even his wife or his civilian friends. Most people couldn't imagine someone like Michael Giles, or that the real world—a cop's world—could be worse than even the bloodiest horror movie. Outsiders couldn't understand what it was like to put aside what he'd seen and heard, or was feeling, and speak to a monster like Giles as if he were a friend. He could talk to another cop about "the job," or he could internalize it, which he knew wasn't healthy, but it wasn't something he could share with anyone else. So he bottled it up, tried to file it away in some dark recess, and forget about it.

The Giles case also taught him that witnesses couldn't be counted on to tell the truth, not even if it was for their benefit. Whether it was Smiley Johnson protecting her great-grandson, or the young black woman who would rather let her attacker off the hook than admit she was wrong, human beings were motivated by a variety of not necessarily logical factors. He would have to keep that in mind as he went forward with his career.

Dealing with Michael Giles also strengthened Sweet's belief that he'd been given a special gift with which to combat evil—a knack for disguising his determination to see justice get served behind a calm, friendly persona that convinced even conscienceless monsters like Giles to relax. The point was reinforced about six months after Giles was sentenced when the teen's mother called him. She said she'd just talked to her son and he wanted to know when Sweet planned to visit him in prison, as if they were friends or connected by some sort of weird bond. The truth was that behind the façade, Sweet would have liked to have reached across the table and strangled Giles during his confession.

It was all part of a detective's learning process. And for Sweet, it would someday seem that his involvement in the Giles case was part of a journey leading to a confrontation with the kind of evil psychopath who would make Giles seem tame by comparison. He hadn't realized it at the time, but walking into the Garland Police Department murder closet in 1996 had been the first step along that road, and two years later a simple phone call would be another.

In the summer of 1998, the crimes against persons bureau office was configured as a big open room with the detectives' desks ringing the walls. When a call from the outside came in to the department receptionist, she would go down the alphabetical list of detectives and pass it to the first detective she got to answer the telephone. Because Sweet was near the end of the list, if he was alone in the office, he'd hear her try one desk, then another, and several more before reaching him.

On this particular day, Sweet was alone, although not by coincidence as much as habit. Early in his career when he was a school resource officer, he'd started eating lunch at 11 a.m. and then going back to work at 12 o'clock to be with the kids. He'd continued the habit as a detective, eating early and then having the office to himself when the other detectives and supervisors went to lunch at noon. It gave him some quiet time to catch up on work and an extra hour on the computer he shared with another detective.

However, this time habit crossed paths with fate, as the telephone rang at first one empty desk and then the next, until finally reaching Sweet. When he answered, the woman on the other end of the line identified herself as Tammy Lopez. She said she was calling in regard to the murder of her daughter Roxann.

It took a moment for Sweet to realize that he was speaking to Roxann Reyes' mother, who at the time of her daughter's disappearance had been Tammy Reyes. But once it clicked, there was no need for her to further explain who she was; even if he hadn't leafed through the files in the murder closet two years earlier, there wasn't an officer on the Garland police force who didn't know the case. Roxann was the first child-abduction murder in the city's history, and it stuck in every Garland cop's craw that her killer had never been caught. He immediately let the woman know that he was familiar with what happened to her daughter and asked what he could do to help.

"I heard there was some new information about my daughter's murder," Tammy replied hopefully.

Sweet was at a loss. He didn't know of anything new. But there were six other detectives, plus their supervisors, in the bureau; it was possible, he told her, that he hadn't heard about a break in the case. "Let me talk to the other detectives," he said, "and I'll get back to you."

When the others returned from lunch, Sweet asked if anybody had new information on the Roxann Reyes case but drew a blank. He called Tammy Lopez back and apologized that there was nothing to report.

After they hung up, Sweet kept hearing the sad, desperate tone of the woman's voice. More than ten years had passed since some unknown killer had murdered her little girl, but her grief was still palpable, and the lack of resolution hung over her like a poisonous fog. He would never forget the sound of her voice as she asked questions for which he had no answers.

CHAPTER SEVEN

June 27, 2000

Two years later, habit and fate would intersect a second time. Sweet was again sitting alone in the office during the lunch hour when the telephone at one of the other detectives' desks jingled. Unanswered, it fell silent; then a telephone on another unmanned desk rang.

He was no longer a rookie with the crimes against persons bureau, but a seasoned vet who'd investigated hundreds of violent crimes and dozens of murders and had never lost a case he'd filed with the District Attorney's Office in Dallas. But no matter how many cases he closed, his desk was always cluttered with files he was currently working on, leaving only enough room for a few photographs of his family.

As the unanswered telephone call jumped back and forth across the room from desk to desk, Sweet found it mildly amusing to check off the names of the detectives who preceded him alphabetically. Whoever was calling obviously hadn't specifically asked for him, and yet as he waited for the call to make its way inexorably to the telephone on which he rested his right hand, it was as if he was being sought out for some task he'd already been chosen to complete.

"Criminal Investigations, this is Detective Sweet."

"There's a Detective Teft from Fort Worth PD on

the line," the receptionist replied.

"Thank you, transfer the call to me." He had no idea who Detective Teft was or wanted; he assumed the Fort Worth detective might want help locating a suspect or a witness in Garland.

When the call was patched through, a woman introduced herself as Det. Diane Teft. She said she'd been in contact with an Ohio prison inmate named Jeffrey Sunnycalb regarding the case of Julie Fuller, a 14-year-old girl from the Fort Worth area who on June 23, 1983, had been abducted and murdered. Sunnycalb had written her a letter saying that a former cellmate, David Elliot Penton, had indicated that Julie was one of his victims.

Teft said she followed up with a telephone call to Sunnycalb in prison, during which he told her that he and Penton had lived together for three years while incarcerated at Warren Correctional Facility near Lebanon, Ohio. Both men were housed in a segregated section of the prison for sex offenders to keep them safe from other prisoners.

Apparently, Penton liked to spend his time boasting about abducting, raping, and murdering little girls all over the country. One of them was Julie Fuller, but Penton supposedly had also named three other Texas victims: Christi Meeks from Mesquite, Christie Proctor from Plano, and Roxann Reyes from Garland.

Sweet's detective radar flipped on at the mention of an inmate from Ohio named David Penton and recalled that day he first looked through the Roxann Reyes file boxes in the murder closet and saw Penton's name on the list of possible suspects. He'd continued to think of Roxann often throughout the two years since her mother called, the heartbroken woman's voice haunting him. He also recognized the names Christi Meeks and Christie Proctor.

The Fort Worth detective said she'd arranged to speak to Sunnycalb by telephone the next morning and wanted to know if someone from the Garland Police Department wanted to be present. Sweet immediately said he would and thanked her for calling. As soon as his supervisor, Lt. Mitch Bates, returned from lunch, Sweet asked for permission to pursue the lead.

"Shoot, yeah," Bates replied. "In fact, I'll go with you."

The next day, Sweet, Bates, and Det. Charles Rene left early for the forty-mile drive to Forth Worth. A tall, slender officer with sandy blond hair, Bates was smart and a good family man; they were friends and had worked the night shift together and as school resource officers. Rene was a tall, athletic, black officer from Lake Charles, Louisiana, and a devout Christian. Sweet had been one of his training officers, and they often worked together on cases. Two years earlier, a few months after the Tammy Lopez call, Sweet had introduced then-rookie detective Rene to the murder closet and the Reyes case. So now he'd suggested that Rene accompany them to Fort Worth.

On the way, the three officers agreed that because Sweet was the most familiar with the details of the case, he would do the talking for the Garland contingent. After getting Bates' go-ahead, Sweet had gone down to the murder closet and brought the Reyes case files up to his desk. He'd then spent several hours familiarizing himself with the details of the case, particularly the information about Penton.

Arriving at the Fort Worth Police Department, the three Garland officers were met by Teft, an older detective nearing retirement age who worked in the sex crimes unit. She led them to her desk, where they were discussing their respective cases when the telephone rang. On the other end of the line was Jeffrey Sunnycalb calling collect from the Ohio prison.

The inmate's time on the telephone was limited to ten minutes, so Teft quickly asked a few follow-up questions about her case and then turned the telephone over to Sweet. He dove right in, asking Sunnycalb if Penton discussed any details about the Reyes case.

Providing details that only the killer and those who investigated the crime should know was the first test of an informant's reliability. Sunnycalb got Sweet's attention when he said that Penton told him he'd abducted Roxann from a field behind an apartment complex in Garland. Of course, that had been reported in the media and could have been seen by Sunnycalb or Penton, but it was an obscure detail repeated thirteen years after the incident. Sweet felt his heart start to beat a bit faster.

Then Sunnycalb claimed that his cellmate boasted about keeping the little girl in his van for three days, repeatedly raping her, before he strangled her. After that, Penton told him that he threw her body over a fence into a wooded field near rural Murphy, Texas.

Again, Sunnycalb's information was accurate and noteworthy. Although there were only skeletal remains, the cause of death was "assumed" to be strangulation or asphyxiation because there was no evidence of gun, knife, or blunt trauma wounds. The inmate's knowledge about the location of the body was even more interesting; the tiny burg of Murphy wasn't exactly the sort of name someone would draw out of a hat. The informant had even added a detail to what was known; Roxann's skeletal remains weren't found for a year after she disappeared, so there was no evidence remaining of sexual assault, but it had been assumed.

"Did he say what she was wearing?" Sweet asked.

"A purple top and pink shorts," Sunnycalb responded.

Sweet was careful not to react too much. He didn't want the informant reading his response and adjusting his story accordingly. But the detective was excited; the description of Roxann's clothing was withheld from the media, but Sunnycalb was spot on.

Sunnycalb said that Penton also bragged about abducting and murdering Christie Proctor and Christi Meeks. That, too, fit with the theory that the Proctor, Meeks, and Reyes cases were connected.

Then the informant added to the intrigue. Penton, he said, also described murdering a fourth child in Van Zandt County in northeast Texas. The Van Zandt County case didn't ring a bell with Sweet, but he didn't doubt that when he got a chance to look it up, he'd find it.

Sunnycalb had not missed yet. The question was whether the informant or Penton was making it all up— that one or the other had somehow learned these details through the media or someone on the outside and was using them for his own ends.

Unfortunately, there wasn't time to get much more out of Sunnycalb. An automated voice broke into their conversation noting that the call would be terminated in one minute. Sweet gave Sunnycalb his telephone number at the Garland Police Department and asked him to call the next day. The automated voice noted that there were ten seconds left, and then the line went dead.

Placing the receiver down, Sweet turned to the others. "I'm pretty excited," he admitted. "He knows details about the case that weren't released to the public."

Sweet's enthusiasm rubbed off on Teft; after all, if Sunnycalb was right about the Reyes case, it boded well for her own. She noted that she had DNA evidence taken from her victim that had just been sent off to a laboratory for comparison to Penton's DNA. If it came back positive, it could break all of the cases wide open.

In the meantime, her agency was sponsoring a meeting among any Texas law enforcement agencies with unsolved cases of missing or murdered children during the period of time Penton might have been in the area. Sweet said he'd be there.

A month later, on July 6, Sweet and Capt. Jody Lay, who headed the Garland PD Criminal Investigations Department, drove back to Fort Worth for the meeting at the Fort Worth Police Academy. Since that first conversation, Sweet had spoken to Sunnycalb a couple of times to clear up a few items. He'd also looked into Sunnycalb's background, and what he found out nauseated him.

Teft had told him that Sunnycalb was a sex offender, but she hadn't told him the details. He'd since learned that the would-be informant had "purchased" an eight-year-old girl from her parents for a case of beer and carton of cigarettes. He then brought her to his mobile home and made her his "wife," even creating a marriage license on his computer. Sunnycalb was eventually caught and convicted for sexual assault on a minor and did a short stint in prison. When he got out, he located the girl again and moved her back in with him. He was caught and convicted again, and this time the judge sentenced him to twenty years.

Knowing that Sunnycalb was a pedophile made Sweet's skin crawl. But as he'd learned from dealing with the likes of Michael Giles and a long list of other criminals, he had to put aside his true feelings and pretend to be a friend to gain Sunnycalb's trust and find out what he needed to know.

Walking into an auditorium at the police academy, Sweet wasn't sure what to expect. He knew that Teft had sent out a teletype to Texas law enforcement agencies regarding the purpose of the meeting, as well as information about Sunnycalb and a timeline of Penton's known whereabouts as best as could be determined. But he was surprised at the large turnout of lawmen representing city police departments, county sheriff's offices, and even the Texas Rangers.

Among those attending was Sgt. Mike Bradshaw of the Mesquite Police Department, an experienced detective and someone Sweet considered a friend. He was representing his agency's interest in the Christi Meeks case. However, as far as Sweet could tell, no one was present from the Plano Police Department regarding the Christie Proctor abduction and murder. He wondered why but thought that perhaps the investigators there knew something he didn't.

One by one, the officers present stood and spoke briefly about their cases, a sad litany of unsolved child abductions and murders. With the memory of Tammy Lopez's voice in his head, Sweet knew that each case file represented a family's torment and the lack of justice. When it was his turn, Sweet gave a quick review of what he knew about the Reyes case, including that David Penton had been listed as a possible suspect. He also noted the details that Sunnycalb had provided that matched the evidence, which he thought made it worth paying attention to what the inmate had to say.

However, he quickly learned, some of the other lawmen present already knew about both Penton and

Sunnycalb, and they weren't impressed. Several said that Penton had once been a suspect in their cases, too, but no one had been able to make a case against him or place him in the area at the time of the abductions.

The meeting concluded with Teft informing the others that she would let them know the results of the DNA testing as soon as they came in. If it came back a positive match for Penton, then Sunnycalb's credibility would improve. If not, perhaps the description of him as untrustworthy was accurate.

Five days later, Detective Teft called with bad news. The DNA comparison was negative. Penton was not her killer. "We're done," she said. She wasn't going to take Sunnycalb's calls anymore.

Mike Bradshaw also called Sweet to say he was dropping out. He said he'd questioned Sunnycalb in the past, and he just didn't trust the guy. For one thing, he said, sometimes they'd be talking and suddenly Sunnycalb would clam up, or it would take him awhile to answer a question, as if he had to think it through. But more damning was that Bradshaw had learned that Sunnycalb had put in an "open records" request to obtain information about the Texas cases. "The guy read about all this stuff he's telling us. I'm just not dealing with him anymore."

Sweet thought about what Bradshaw said. The sergeant was older and more experienced, as were many of the investigators from the other agencies who believed that Sunnycalb was just another lying convict. Maybe they were right; between being wrong about the Julie Fuller case and the open records revelation, it didn't look good.

Still, Sweet wasn't quite ready to give up. Maybe it was his inexperience; maybe he was just being naïve and hoping that the information would turn out to be true so that he could bring some closure to Roxann's family. But it also felt like it was something he had to see to the end, that a greater power was pushing him, and he couldn't let it go.

"I think I'm going to keep talking to him," Sweet told Bradshaw.

There was a pause on the other end of the line, and then Bradshaw said, "Good for you. Go for it; it will be a good learning experience."

CHAPTER EIGHT

July 12, 2000

The next time Sweet spoke to Sunnycalb, he challenged him about his claim that Penton was involved in the Julie Fuller abduction and murder.

"Look at the letter," Sunnycalb retorted. "I didn't say he did it, I said, 'You would do well to consider him.'" He said he'd been trying to check out what Penton was telling him and had found Julie's name on a list of missing children he'd been able to obtain in spite of his incarceration. He'd noticed some resemblance between her murder and Penton's other boasts and thought it was worth bringing to the attention of the Fort Worth police.

After getting off the telephone, Sweet called Det. Teft and asked her to send him a copy of Sunnycalb's letter. When he read it, he saw that the informant had told him the truth; Sunnycalb only suggested that Penton was a possibility due to the similarity and timing of Julie Fuller's murder to the other Texas cases.

Being right about his letter kept Sunnycalb's credibility alive with Sweet. It was the beginning of a long series of telephone calls as Sunnycalb fed him information in bits and pieces.

During one of the first calls, Sweet asked Sunnycalb how the topic of murdering children had first come up with Penton. "We were watching the Oprah Winfrey show about the Christie Proctor case," Sunnycalb recalled. "It was almost like he went into a trance when they started talking about it; then he started correcting the facts that they were getting wrong. That's when he told me he did it."

Sunnycalb said that Penton preferred certain kinds of victims. He liked darker-skinned kids—black, Hispanic and Asian—though he would take what was available; and he targeted low-income areas because "no one would give a shit" if those kids disappeared. He called them "throwaway kids."

Sunnycalb conceded that he knew that Penton was a liar and probably embellished his brutality to impress other inmates. He said that Penton boasted about murdering as many as fifty young girls, beginning in South Korea, where he'd been stationed in the Army, and then throughout the Midwest and South. But judging from the cases in which Penton seemed to know the intimate details, Sunnycalb put the number of Penton's victims at closer to twenty-five.

Sweet was stunned. Even with as much violence and horror as he'd experienced so far in his career, he had a hard time believing that Penton could have killed twenty-five little girls over a period of years.

The number paled in comparison to the world's most prolific known serial child killers, such as three South Americans thought to hold that heinous distinction: Luis "The Beast" Garavito, reported to have raped and killed more than 400 street children; Pedro "The Monster of the Andes" Alonson Lopez, whose victims were said to number more than 300; and Daniel Barbosa, believed to have raped and killed 150. However, in the United States, with its modern law enforcement capabilities and inter-agency communication and computers—especially compared to countries where the disappearance of street children might go unnoticed—twenty-five victims was a staggering number. If true, or even on the low side, it meant that Penton was one of the worst, known serial child killers in U.S. history.

What's more, it meant that Penton committed his crimes at a time when the issue of child abductions and murders was gaining national prominence. In the United States, instigated by infamous child abductions—such as the 1979 kidnapping and murder of six-year-old Etan Patz from New York City and the 1981 abduction and murder of six-year-old Adam Walsh from a Florida shopping mall—efforts to create a national law enforcement response to child abductions led to the creation in 1984 of the National Center for Missing & Exploited Children. Paid for largely by the U.S. Justice Department, the purpose of the center was to become a national clearinghouse and resource for parents, law enforcement agencies, schools, and communities to assist in locating missing children and raise public awareness. The main tool was the FBI's national crime computer to record, track, and share information, which previously were all efforts hampered by jurisdictional lines.

Other cases would make their way into the national consciousness about what had previously been a hidden epidemic, including that of Shannon Sherrill, the six-year-old whose October 1986 disappearance from her mother's yard in Thorntown, Indiana, had become a national story even in those days before the internet. In Texas, relatives of Christi Meeks worked to bring widespread attention to her disappearance by establishing the Christi Meeks Foundation for Missing Children, which helped get the girl's picture on billboards, milk cartons, and flyers.

However, some killers were better at flying under the radar than others, and it was difficult to link crimes committed in one state with those in another. Sunnycalb noted that Penton sometimes changed his stories a little bit, or seemed to mix up names, or didn't always know the name of every victim he claimed to have raped and murdered.

But Penton was consistent and specific about some cases, and for those reasons, Sunnycalb was absolutely convinced that his former cellmate was responsible for the murders of Meeks, Proctor, and Reyes. He told Sweet that Penton referred to the girls by name and knew minute details, such as the clothes they'd been wearing, the dates and locations of their abductions, and where their bodies were left.

Penton bragged about being smarter than the cops, Sunnycalb said. He claimed to be very meticulous when hunting for victims, lurking around schools and areas where children played, waiting for the right opportunity to strike fast, and then be away before anyone noticed. He even scouted the areas where he planned to murder the girls and dump their bodies, taking his victims from one jurisdiction into another to confuse law enforcement efforts. He smirked when he boasted about his crimes and said he would have never been caught except he'd make a mistake in Ohio when he killed Nydra Ross because he knew her uncle and had been seen with her.

It was this tendency to boast, Sweet realized, that was Penton's fatal flaw. He enjoyed recounting his atrocities, reliving them over and over in graphic detail. No matter what the topic of discussion was in the beginning, Sunnycalb told him, it wouldn't take Penton long to turn the conversation around to the little girls he'd abducted, raped, and murdered. He liked being the center of attention and seemed to "get off" sexually by regaling other inmates with each horrific detail. Such a proclivity for bragging could come back to haunt him.

When the Sunnycalb described how Penton relished recalling the murders, Sweet was reminded of Michael Giles and how he liked to relive his crimes over and over while sitting on the roof of his great-grandmother's house. There was a similarity to their evil—the calculated, remorseless infliction of fear, suffering, and death on defenseless victims—though if Sunnycalb was right about the numbers, Penton was much further along in his career as a murderous psychopath.

Penton had never satisfied his deviant bloodlust. He told any inmate who'd listen that he hoped to someday get out of prison and resume his atrocities. Sunnycalb recalled how sometimes they'd be watching television and a young girl would appear on the screen. "He'd make comments like, 'She better be glad I'm in here, or I would have her.'"

The killer had even decided to change tactics. In the past, he'd sometimes punched his small victims in the stomach to knock the wind out of them and prevent them from screaming or struggling as he carried them to his vehicle. Now if he ever got another chance, he said he'd use an electric stun device to disable them.

Sweet checked with Ohio authorities and found out Penton would be eligible for parole in 2027 for his conviction in the Nydra Ross case, which would make him about 69 years old. He'd still be capable of preying on little girls. Of course, as sometimes happened in an uncertain justice system, he also could be released early or sent to a less-secure facility, where he could escape. If he got out, it might be tough to catch him again, too.

After all, he'd disappeared following his conviction for the death of his infant son and avoided detection for four years, during which time, if Sunnycalb's information was correct, he'd murdered three little girls in Texas and one in Ohio.

At least, Sweet thought, *and probably many more than that.* He believed it was his responsibility to make sure Penton never got out of prison again. Or better yet, Texas was a state that often sought and carried out the death penalty. He could think of no better end for a child killer than to be strapped to a gurney, pumped full of poison, and put down like a mad dog.

So far in their conversations, Sunnycalb had proved to be reliable, but Sweet still cautioned himself to be skeptical. He asked Sunnycalb about Mesquite Det. Mike Bradshaw's complaint that sometimes during their telephone conversations he clammed up, or wouldn't answer a question directly, or he'd start talking completely off the subject. But Sunnycalb had an explanation. The prison telephone he used didn't allow for any privacy, and he had to be guarded in what he said if other inmates approached. *"Snitches get stitches or end up in ditches"* was not just a saying when living in a penitentiary setting.

Once again, Sunnycalb's reasoning made sense, and Sweet wondered why so many other officers thought that the informant couldn't be trusted. He discovered that the main source of the aspersions was Det. Keith Grisham with the Plano Police Department, the agency involved in the Proctor case. So he called and reached the detective. Grisham was nearing retirement, but he said he'd be happy to help, including discussing Sunnycalb and the Proctor case.

When they met, Grisham repeated what he'd

been telling other law enforcement officers, including an FBI agent looking into a case in the Midwest. He stated flat out that Sunnycalb was a liar. He said that in 1998, he'd received a letter from Sunnycalb saying he had information about the three Dallas-area murders. So Grisham arranged for Sunnycalb to be transferred into a county jail in Ohio so that they could meet him without other prison inmates knowing. Then he and Det. Billy Meeks, also of the Plano Police Department and no relation to Christi Meeks, had flown to Ohio to interview him.

"He didn't tell me shit," Grisham explained to Sweet. "I got my department's approval and flew all the way up there and had to come back with nothing. He's a flake, and I think he was just playing with us." If Sweet wanted to waste his time listening to Sunnycalb, it was up to him.

In spite of his feeling about Sunnycalb, Grisham was helpful. He told Sweet everything he could about the Proctor murder in case it would help. He even took Sweet to the dirt road in a wooded area near Plano where Christie Proctor's body was found, and then to the field near Murphy, Texas, both of them in Collin County, where Roxann's body had been dumped.

Later, Sweet asked Sunnycalb about Grisham's complaints about the interview in Ohio. The informant didn't try to hide his annoyance. He said that when Grisham asked to interview him, he'd agreed on two conditions: He didn't want to be videotaped, or for anything to be written down. "I said that I'd tell him everything I knew," Sunnycalb explained. But worried about being identified as a snitch, he didn't want anyone to have proof that he'd talked.

Grisham agreed to the conditions, Sunnycalb said,

and everything went well with the interview until the detective said he needed a smoke break. He and Meeks then left Sunnycalb alone in the interview room. But they didn't realize that Sunnycalb was an electrician by trade, and when he saw the coaxial wires used for videotaping coming out of a speaker box in the corner, he knew he'd been betrayed. He got up, walked over to the speaker box and saw the small camera hidden inside. "After I saw the camera, I didn't tell them shit," he said to Sweet.

Sweet was amused that the informant had just used the same description of his interview that Grisham had, only in a different context. Without revealing Sunnycalb's version of what took place at the Ohio prison, he called Grisham and asked if he could view the videotape from the Ohio interview.

Watching the tape was the first time Sweet saw what Sunnycalb looked like—a bald, portly man in his mid-forties who reminded the detective of Mr. Spacely on the old *The Jetsons* cartoon. Just as Sunnycalb had told him, the first part of the interview went off without a hitch. Then when the other detectives left the room, Sunnycalb noticed the speaker box, got up, walked up to the hidden camera and scowled. When the detectives returned, Sunnycalb didn't tell Grisham and Meeks that he knew he'd been lied to; he just sat sullenly and hardly spoke the rest of the meeting.

Once again, Sunnycalb's version of events was accurate, but it had torched his credibility with law enforcement. In the years since his falling out with Grisham, Sunnycalb said, he'd been trying to let law enforcement agencies know about Penton's claims. But no one had responded to his letters and calls until he contacted Diane Teft in Fort Worth. And then, only

Sweet had stuck with him.

Still, if Sweet was going to make a case against Penton, he needed a lot more than the word of a pedophile like Jeffrey Sunnycalb. He was going to have to find other witnesses and evidence to corroborate what the informant had to say.

Sweet knew it was going to be a long, hard road. A lot of time had passed; witnesses disappeared, and memories dimmed; evidence that might have existed in the mid- to late-1980s was likely to have been lost or destroyed. Not only that, but whatever he did, he would have to do in his spare time. His caseload of current crimes wasn't going anywhere, and he couldn't drop them for murders that had happened so long ago that only their families and maybe a few old-timer cops remembered. Still, if he wouldn't answer the call to bring these cases to a close for the families and for the victims, who would?

CHAPTER NINE

A few days later ...

Walking down the stairs to the murder closet, Sweet pulled the Reyes case file boxes from the shelves. He knew the first time he'd looked in the boxes that the contents were a disorganized mess. He loaded them into his car and drove to the small town where he and his family lived in a quiet, middle-class neighborhood of brick homes, many of them owned by cops and firefighters.

In his living room, Sweet turned the boxes over and dumped them on the floor. Out of curiosity, his wife, Julie, began looking through some of the photographs and came across one of a clump of dark hair with a little girl's hair clasp still attached. It was a horrible reminder of what had happened to the child, and she had to walk away.

It was a photograph that got to Sweet: an image of little Roxann sharing a kiss with her father as they played on the living room floor of their home. He couldn't help but put himself and his three daughters into that photograph and choked up. The case had become personal.

Sweet set the photograph of Roxann and her father aside and looked down at the jumbled piles of paper that represented the Roxann Reyes homicide investigation as it had been left by the detective originally assigned to the case. He had tried talking to the now-retired detective, but he wasn't interested in helping and didn't have much to say. He'd just given up and dumped it all in the two boxes to be stored in the murder closet.

Getting down on his hands and knees, Sweet picked up a sheet of paper, read it, and placed it on a clear spot on the carpet. In that manner, he scanned every single note, receipt, and telephone message, every photograph and sketch. Then, he organized them. Items that at least *seemed* important to him—such as statements from several people, including Penton's sister, taken by the Columbus Police Department, and a car title for a gray, four-door Datsun sedan—he placed in separate files according to subject matter; they would go into one of the boxes. The items that didn't make sense to him he filed and consigned to the second box, unless, and until, they became relevant.

Sometimes it was difficult to tell which box some bit of information belonged in. For instance, when he read the offense report for the Roxann Reyes case, a potential witness by the name of Wanda Huggins who lived in the same apartment complex was mentioned. She'd told police that she'd seen a man matching the description given by Roxann's friend, Julia Diaz, wandering through the complex. She said that when she made eye contact with the stranger, he turned and ran. If true, Huggins might have been able to identify the attacker from a photo lineup, but there was nothing in the file to indicate if anyone had followed up on her report.

When he was done organizing, Sweet went back and read it all again, this time more carefully. He wanted to learn every detail he could about the Reyes case so that when Sunnycalb told him new information, he'd know whether the evidence corroborated it.

Like a hunter sizing up the animal he intended to pursue, Sweet also wanted to know everything he could about Penton. He learned that David Elliot Penton was born Feb. 9, 1958, and raised in Columbus, Ohio, and that his father had walked out on him, his mother, and sister when Penton was a child.

After dropping out of high school in 1977, he joined the Army, arriving at Fort Hood near Killeen, Texas, in Bell County in the fall. He soon married a young woman from Ohio named Katherine, who happened to be the daughter of the man married to Penton's mother. Katherine, who had a young daughter from a previous relationship, moved with him to Killeen, where she gave birth to another girl.

While stationed at Fort Hood, they owned a brown Fury two-door sedan and white Plymouth van. The marriage didn't last, and the couple divorced in 1979. When they parted, Penton kept the van with its distinctive brown stripes on the side.

In February 1980, Penton married his second wife, a Korean national named Kyong, and three months later was transferred to Korea. Trained as a track vehicle mechanic, he was also an expert marksman and deemed "highly motivated" by his superiors, who promoted him to sergeant. However, he was charged with storing alcohol in his foot locker, then a few months later with lying about his marital status to obtain unearned benefits, and was demoted to specialist.

In June 1981, the Army transferred Penton back to Fort Hood for a year before shipping him off to Korea again. When his tour was up in September 1983, Penton returned to Texas with his wife and their baby girl; a year later, the couple had a baby boy they named Michael.

In November 1984, Penton was arrested for killing

his two-month-old son. The county medical examiner determined that he violently shook the child in a "fit of rage" because the infant would not stop crying.

In May 1985, Penton pleaded guilty to manslaughter and was discharged from the Army. But he appealed for a delay in his sentencing and was allowed out on bond. He then fled Texas, and disappeared, until he was arrested in Ohio three years later for the murder of Nydra Ross.

It was during those three years between Penton being charged with his son's death and his arrest for the murder of Nydra that three little girls were abducted and murdered in the Dallas area: Christi Meeks in January 1985; Christie Proctor in February 1986; and Roxann Reyes in November 1987. There was nothing in the evidence box that indicated they knew the man who took them. However, nine-year-old Nydra had met the bogeyman before he killed her.

Penton worked with her uncle, who she'd gone to visit in Columbus, and he'd been at that home on the evening of March 30, 1988. The next day, when no one was looking, he forced Nydra into his van, where he drove her to a remote location, then raped and strangled her. He then drove across the county line into a rural part of Marion County east of the small town of Waldo. He'd been there before, scouting the lay of the land and picking a spot where a small creek cut through a heavily wooded ravine running parallel to the dirt road he drove down. He stopped, then after making sure no one was around, he pulled the body from his van and threw her into the dense brush. Satisfied for the moment, he drove back to Columbus.

Nydra's uncle reported her missing, and a search was launched. Penton even helped, but it didn't take long for him to become a suspect. He'd made a mistake;

instead of driving somewhere far away and abducting a child he didn't know, he'd struck too close to home and was seen with Nydra before she disappeared.

Even more damning, a large bloodstain was discovered on the carpet beneath one of the seats in Penton's van. However, DNA blood-typing was still in its infancy and not available at the time to the investigators with the Marion County Sheriff's Office. So while it was highly suspicious—and not something Penton could easily explain away—it wasn't enough to arrest him. Not yet.

Taken from her family, brutalized and murdered by a monster, and then disposed of like trash, Nydra Ross went missing for six months. Then that fall, a hunter stumbling through the foliage near the stream happened upon a human skeleton.

The Marion County coroner quickly determined that the remains had been exposed to the elements as long as six months and that they belonged to a black girl, around ten years old, who stood four foot six inches. Investigators with the county sheriff's office surmised that at long last, Nydra had been found. But to be sure, they took bone marrow and blood samples from Nydra's mother and sent them to a lab in New York to be compared to the remains. It took until January 1989 to get the results, but they were conclusive: The murdered child was Nydra Ross.

Even then, Penton wasn't indicted and charged with aggravated murder and kidnapping until May 1990, as the Columbus PD homicide detectives meticulously put their case together. Penton's trial started April 4, 1991, more than three-and-a-half years after Nydra's body was found. He faced the death penalty in Ohio's electric chair if convicted.

Prosecutors in the case had several pieces of evidence to work with, including that he was the last person seen with her and the bloodstain found in his van. But the most critical, perhaps, was the testimony of several men who were in jail with Penton after he was arrested. Each took the stand and testified about what the suspect told them; their stories were similar enough to corroborate one another and yet different enough to not sound rehearsed. One said Penton told him that he'd talked Nydra into climbing into his van, where he then raped and strangled her. The other testified that Penton told him that when he attempted to have sex with the child, she resisted, so he'd struck her. At that point, Penton realized he couldn't let her go, so he killed her.

A little more than two weeks after the trial began, it ended with the jurors convicting Penton for aggravated murder and kidnapping. He then faced a second trial to determine if his crime met the legal justifications for him to be put to death.

As with most states that have the death penalty, Ohio law required the second trial so that jurors could weigh so-called "aggravating factors" against "mitigating factors." Presented by the prosecution through witness testimony and evidence, aggravating factors are circumstances about the crime that raise it to a level above other similar crimes, such as premeditation, evidence that the crime was committed to cover-up another crime, like rape, or that the murder was particularly "cruel, heinous, or depraved." Oftentimes, evidence prohibited at the guilt/innocence trial—such as the defendant's previous criminal history, or "victim impact" statements from family members—will come into play. Among those who testified against Penton in this phase were his two ex-wives, who said that he'd sexually molested his own daughters.

After the prosecution has presented the aggravating factors, the defense then presents any mitigating circumstances. These can range from whether the defendant was using drugs or alcohol at the time of the crime, suffered from a brain injury or was mentally deficient, or was subjected to a particularly difficult childhood that impacted his ability to control himself or judge right from wrong. The jurors are then asked to determine if the mitigating circumstances outweigh the aggravating factors, and if not, whether the defendant "deserves" to die for the crime.

Unlike some states, such as Texas, where the death penalty is a realistic possibility, prosecutors in Ohio didn't often win those fights. In the end, the Penton jury decided that the aggravating factors did not outweigh the mitigating circumstances, thus Penton escaped the electric chair. Instead, he was sentenced to life with the possibility of parole, which he began serving at the Marion Correctional Institute.

As he familiarized himself with the Ross case, Sweet noted the similarities to his investigation, not just the *modus operandi* of the crime—the pattern of Penton's kidnapping, rape, and strangulation of young girls—but also his behavior afterwards. In the Nydra Ross case, Penton had crossed jurisdictional lines, abducting the child in Columbus and then driving all the way into a rural part of Marion County before leaving the body in a wooded area, where it wasn't found for months. If, as Sweet suspected, Penton was the killer in Texas, he'd followed the same pattern: taking his victims from one place and leaving them in another remote area, where the possibility of immediate discovery was remote.

The Ross case also corroborated Sunnycalb's

assertion that Penton was obsessed with talking about his crimes. Instead of keeping his mouth shut, he'd almost immediately started bragging to other inmates in the Marion County jail. Sweet hoped that if he'd been so eager to boast about the Ross case and then to discuss other murders with Sunnycalb, Penton may have also discussed the Texas cases with other Ohio inmates. He put that aside as something to follow up on.

Hoping to locate someone in law enforcement who could further shed some light on Penton's possible connection to the Texas cases, Sweet called the police department in Columbus, Ohio. Detective Rick Sheasby had retired, but another detective gave Sweet his home telephone number to call.

Sheasby was more than happy to talk to him about Penton. "I know he's good for more than the Nydra Ross murder," he said. He'd pegged Penton as a serial killer from the start, and Roxann's grandparents had confirmed it, as far as Sheasby was concerned. Penton, of course, had denied it.

Although he'd contacted Texas police agencies several times about his suspicions, Sheasby said it never went anywhere. He told Sweet he should look at the transcript of the interview between Penton's then-28-year-old sister, Amanda, and Columbus PD Det. Rita Doberneck. The interview was conducted at Amanda's home in Waynoka, Oklahoma, on August 11, 1988, more than a month before Nydra Ross's body was found.

Sweet was aware of the transcript, which he'd spotted in the Reyes case files. After speaking to Sheasby, he went back to review it. According to the document, Amanda told Doberneck that their father, Lathern Penton, disappeared two months before she was born. *"He left for work and was never heard from again."* Her grandmother then moved in with the family and helped raise the children until her death in 1976; her mother then remarried a year later.

Amanda told the detective that her brother, who was two years older, was her mother's favorite. She said he'd been thrown out of a car in an accident when he was six months old and was in a coma for a time. He made a slow recovery and needed special care for so long that her mother once told her it was like raising two babies at once after Amanda was born. She attributed her brother's higher place in her mother's affections to his special needs. *"David could do no wrong in my mother's eyes, and if it was between me and David, I could do no right."*

At first, her brother was behind other children in school, but soon caught up and became an "A" student. However, it didn't last. *"Almost overnight"* his personality changed when he became a teenager; he began skipping school, and his grades dropped. He turned violent and was abusive towards his sister; his moods fluctuated wildly and without warning—calm one moment, agitated the next. Amanda recalled an incident when she'd come home from school and was standing at the top of the stairs in their home when her brother entered. *"He looked at me with a wild look in his eyes. Then, he ran up the stairs and grabbed me and hung me over the banister. He did these things to me often."* She said that although Penton abused her physically, he never sexually molested her.

Penton dropped out of school after failing a grade and realizing he would be in the same class as his sister. *"He couldn't handle that."* So he joined the Army.

According to Amanda, her brother's main male role model from the time he was about six until he left for the Army was a man he met through the Big Brother organization. The man took him camping and even on a trip to see the man's mother in Washington, D.C. That man, according to Amanda, never married.

Although the Army described Penton as a motivated soldier, Amanda told the detective that his personality continued to change for the worse while in the service. He became more violent and prone to fits of rage. His vicious temper and *"sadistic"* nature carried over to his wife, Katherine.

"David used to beat her in front of me. He did mean things to her. One day it was 110 degrees in Texas, and she was nine months pregnant; he drove her away in the car and forced her out. She had to walk all the way back home, and he locked her out."

Amanda claimed that her brother molested Katherine's daughter from her first marriage, and that his wife left him when he molested their own infant daughter. He then married Kyong.

After David Penton was discharged from the Army and on the run from authorities in Texas for the murder of his son, Amanda said, he moved back to Columbus, Ohio, into his mother's home. Amanda and her husband, Andrew, were also living in Columbus at the time, and the two men worked together. Penton did the driving, and on the way home after work, he liked to cruise past elementary schools and playgrounds to watch the children. *"He would point out various children to Andrew."*

In January 1987, Amanda and her husband moved to Oklahoma and felt relieved to be away from her brother because of concerns about their own children. *"I believe David is capable of hurting children. I believe that David did murder those children in Texas,"* she told

Doberneck. *"I just hope you can prove it and get him locked up. I will not take my children to Columbus while David is there. So if you charge him with these murders, and he goes to prison for it, I hope you will let me know so that I can visit Columbus again. I don't want my children around him; I don't want them molested."*

Amanda told Doberneck that her mother would never cooperate with the police. *"She will always protect David no matter what."* She said she was aware that her mother's husband had been cooperating with the police, but neither of them wanted her mother to know that they were talking to the authorities. However, she told the detective that she would help investigators if she could and would call if she thought of anything else that might be important.

After reading through the transcript, Sweet called Amanda, hoping to ask a few questions of his own. She was back living in Columbus, Ohio, with her mother, and he hoped that with her brother in prison, she wouldn't be afraid to talk. But she claimed that she couldn't even remember being interviewed by Doberneck and denied that she'd ever said anything negative about her sibling. Instead, she claimed that her brother had visited her in Oklahoma several times, and there'd been no problems involving children—hers or anybody else's.

Hanging up, Sweet was again reminded of the Giles case and what it said about human beings and their motivations. He didn't believe Amanda. Not her claim that she couldn't remember being interviewed by a police detective. Not her denial of having ever accused her brother of any crimes or deviant behavior towards children.

In Sweet's opinion, the Doberneck transcript was too detailed with Penton's personal history that it could have only come from a family member. Nor would it have made sense for the Columbus detective to create a story out of whole cloth and attribute it to a potentially important witness. How would Doberneck have even known enough to make up that Amanda's husband and brother used to cruise elementary schools to watch children play? Or that Amanda and her husband had moved to Oklahoma to get away from her brother?

Sweet suspected that Amanda's denials stemmed from the fact that she was living in Columbus. The transcript made it obvious that she was afraid of her brother and wasn't going to cross her mother, who believed that her son *"could do no wrong."*

Replacing the interview document in the box, Sweet dug up other papers associated with the Ohio case. He found an assessment created by an FBI profiler, who'd labeled Penton a *"sexual sadist"* with a high IQ who collected pornography. He was likely *"to have been sexually abused before the age of ten. ... and lives with his mother, parents, or an older woman."*

Penton *"likes Asians because they are from a submissive society and will go along with bizarre sex acts (and children will). ... Intimidates women in relationships by threats of violence, instills fear through bizarre sex."*

As a killer, Penton would be *"neat, methodical, premeditated ... who sets up the fantasy in his mind and acts when he finds a victim to fit it. But does not stalk the victim—is opportunist. ... He will not risk kidnapping a victim who will resist; will entice and lure them quietly away if others are around. "* He would act alone: *"likes violence, would not share."*

Penton would also engage in anal intercourse and bondage *"because his sexual thrill is fear of the victim."*

He would not kill the victim after one sex act, but instead *"take (the) victim to an area where he would feel secure enough to do it repeatedly."* A killer of this sort would carry out his attacks *"in a place very familiar to him, such as a friend's vacant house that he had a key to, (or) a vacant (abandoned) house that he knew about, not a wooded area unless extremely remote."*

When through sexually assaulting his victims, he would *"use methods that leave the least physical evidence—strangulation and suffocation, as opposed to stabbing or gunshot, will not risk cutting the body up unless the place where it is done involves no risk."* Then he would *"dispose of the body in a preplanned place, not haphazardly dump it. ... Will carefully, and methodically, get rid of body, evidence, and cover his tracks."*

There was one piece of evidence Penton might create and keep, according to the profiler. Depending on his finances or access to equipment, he was likely to record or videotape his atrocities in order to re-enact the fantasy.

A clever, pathological liar, Penton would also volunteer to search for the victim *"even to the point of assuming leadership in the search."* He would stay in close contact with the police to monitor the progress of the investigation. *"When interviewed he will interrogate the interrogator on the progress."*

The profiler's assessment stopped short of calling Penton a serial killer because he did not *"strike regularly, such as monthly."*

Sweet was not surprised that the report concluded that pursuing a killer like Penton would be *"one of the most difficult cases to investigate and prove."* But he was convinced that he was working for a higher power and wasn't about to be deterred.

CHAPTER TEN

July 24, 2000

After talking to Sheasby and reviewing the documents from the Ohio investigation, Sweet's next step fell closer to home. He decided it was time to interview Julia Diaz, who'd been picking flowers with Roxann and was chased by her abductor. Although thirteen years had passed, he hoped she would be able to pick that man out of a photo lineup, but first he had to find her.

Signing on to the Garland Police Department records computer, Sweet checked to see if someone named Julia Diaz had any sort of contact with the city. There was no guarantee she still went by that name or lived in the area—she could have married or moved—but it was a start. Nothing came up. So he tried LexisNexis, a company that provided computer-assisted legal research assistance and was more up-to-date with current addresses. This time he was in luck; there was a Julia Diaz who was the right age and still living in Garland.

Sweet drove to the address listed. No one answered the door, so he left his business card. A few hours later, he received a call from a woman who said she was Julia's mother and wanted to know why he was looking for her daughter. After he explained, she said she would have Julia get back to him. It wasn't long before he heard from the young woman. Yes, she said, she was the same person who'd been playing with Roxann Reyes when the man appeared and offered candy.

The next day, accompanied by her mother, the 19-year-old woman walked into the Garland Police Department reception area. Sweet met them and guided them to an interview room, where he talked a little about the status of the case. He then began to question Julia, first asking her to talk about herself to put her at ease.

Short with long, straight, dark hair, Julia Diaz had survived her brush with a killer to become an intelligent, attractive young woman. She said she was working for an insurance company. She was nervous about discussing what had happened, "but I want to help if I can."

Julia said she had never forgotten the terror of the bogeyman chasing her or that he took her little friend away forever. She recalled what happened that day almost exactly as she had described it to a police officer when she was six years old.

Sweet brought with him a photo lineup that included a picture of Penton as he'd looked in the late 1980s. He hoped that she'd be able to pick him out, but she warned him that she wasn't sure she could remember the killer's face; she'd done her best to block it out of her memory. He hesitated; if he showed her the lineup and she couldn't identify Penton, it could cause trouble later at trial. So instead he asked if she would be willing to be hypnotized to help her recall that day, and the man, more clearly.

Although uneasy about it, Julia agreed and a few days later she was hypnotized by Det. Keith Prinz. An experienced forensic hypnotist, Prinz took his time. When Diaz was under, he took her back to when she was six years old and had her describe the apartment she lived in and then the complex itself. Sitting in the room, Sweet was amazed at her detailed descriptions. He had no doubt that she was seeing her childhood home.

Slowly, Prinz brought her up to that fateful day in November 1987 when she was outside playing with Roxann. Suddenly, Julia's mood and demeanor changed; she became visibly upset and didn't want to talk about what happened next. Gently, carefully, Prinz eased off into a more comfortable memory and then brought her forward again. This time, Julia described picking flowers with Roxann in a field across from the apartment complex when a man slowly drove up in a gray, four-door car and began talking to them. Then he got out of his car and asked if they wanted candy.

Prinz asked her to describe the man, starting with his feet. She recalled that he was wearing black running shoes and a gray jogging suit. The hypnotist asked her to look up at the face of the man. She tried, but then her face contorted. It was painful for Sweet just to watch her struggle to see the face of the monster. Then she broke down and began to sob. It was as far as she could go, and Prinz had no choice but to bring her out of it.

When fully awake, Julia wiped at her tears and apologized for stopping when she did. She said she'd be willing to try again some other day.

Sweet assured her that she'd helped a lot. However, he had another idea and suggested that they drive over to the apartment complex where the man in the gray car abducted Roxann. She could then show him what up to that point he'd only seen in photographs.

Arriving at the apartment complex, Sweet noted that where thirteen years earlier it had been a low-rent, crime-ridden haven for drug dealers and prostitutes, it was worse now (and would be torn down in a couple more years). Julia and her family had moved away shortly after Roxann's abduction, but she guided Sweet around as if the attack had taken place only the day before.

There, she pointed, was the field where they'd picked flowers to take to Roxann's mother. And here was the alley where the man in the car had first appeared and then stopped when he saw them. Over there was the small opening between buildings just big enough for a six-year-old girl to run through but not a snarling, angry fiend.

Sweet turned into the alley and drove to the far end from which the man had come that day. When he reached the end, he stopped; they were sitting across the street from an elementary school. He knew in that instant that the killer had once sat there, too, watching the children play, waiting for his chance. On a warm afternoon in November 1987, this had been his hunting ground.

It was good for Sweet to see the scene of the crime as Julia Diaz described the events. He'd discovered that one of the most difficult obstacles to overcome when working a cold case was getting a feel for the environment where the crime occurred. Photos didn't always show what he needed to see, but now he could visualize what had happened. The visit, however, had been hard on Julia, and she cried as he drove her back to the police station.

He thanked her. "I'll be in touch," he said and meant it, though he didn't know when or under what circumstances. Still traumatized, Julia Diaz had blocked the memory of the bogeyman's face from her mind, and he didn't want to risk having his only living eyewitness unable to pick him out of a lineup. Maybe someday she'd be able to get past her mental block, and he might try again.

In the meantime, Diaz had confirmed some of the information she'd given to police investigators as a child, particularly her detailed description of the suspect's car. Just small pieces of a large puzzle, but they might someday prove invaluable.

CHAPTER ELEVEN

August 2, 2000

As the weeks passed following that first telephone call from Det. Teft, Sweet felt himself drawn further and further into the case, as though pulled or pushed by an unseen force. And in the center of it all was Jeffrey Sunnycalb, pedophile and informant, who called sometimes three or four times a day.

Talking to him on the telephone was a frustrating, drawn-out process, with each conversation limited to the ten minutes; prison authorities finally agreed to up it to fifteen, but that still limited their discussions, especially with frequent interruptions. As Mike Bradshaw had noted without understanding why, Sunnycalb was guarded in what he said if other inmates approached while he was on the telephone. Penton was still in the same part of the prison, and there was no telling what he would have done, or asked some other inmate to do, if he found out that his former cellie was talking to the police. And for every question answered or new piece of information divulged, it seemed Sweet had a dozen more questions to ask when the automated voice announced that there was a minute left, then thirty seconds, then ten, and then the line would go dead.

Sometimes he wondered if Sunnycalb was holding information back in order to milk the situation; then again, at times Sweet felt so overwhelmed by it all he didn't know if he could have handled more. He had to check everything the informant told him and try to corroborate the details—difficult enough to do when a case is fresh, much tougher when more than a dozen years have passed.

And it wasn't just the three Texas cases Sweet was working on. The more Sweet talked to the informant, the more stories he heard about murders Penton claimed to have committed in other parts of the country. There was a little girl who'd disappeared in Indiana named Shannon Sherrill, and at least two more possible abduction-murders in Texas. In one of the Texas cases, Sunnycalb didn't have a name or exact location, just that Penton bragged about abducting a young black girl from a mobile home somewhere in East Texas. He also said that Penton claimed to have abducted Angelica Marie Gandara, an eleven-year-old girl from Temple, Texas, who disappeared on July 14, 1985.

Sweet was interested in the other cases. He believed that David Penton was as evil and dangerous a man, at least to children, as he'd ever encountered. Penton's behavioral patterns placed him firmly in the category of a monstrous serial killer: the careful stalking and planning; abducting in one place, murdering and dumping in another to avoid apprehension; and the multiple rape-and-strangulation murders. He likely had many other victims, as Sunnycalb claimed.

At first, Sweet tried calling other law enforcement agencies when Sunnycalb told him about each new victim. But most never called him back, or if they did talk to him, they'd blow off what he had to say because it was coming from a prison informant.

In the Gandara case, Sweet contacted the Texas Ranger who'd been assigned to the investigation. Temple was only twenty-five miles from Fort Hood, where Penton was stationed at the time of Angelica's disappearance. Sweet thought that made Penton a good suspect. However, the ranger only sent him his files on the case and wished him "good luck."

Sweet had to make a choice. He was getting far too much information for him to track down these other cases, and he wasn't getting any help. So he decided to concentrate on the three abductions from the Dallas area; the goal was to put Penton away permanently, and to do that he needed to focus on Reyes, Meeks, and Proctor. He continued to take notes about the others, but then he'd redirect Sunnycalb back to the three little girls he could do something about.

Trying to keep up with his regular caseload and Sunnycalb was wearing Sweet out. But he kept accepting the collect calls, including on a dog-day in August when the outside temperature in central Texas was cruising past 100 degrees before noon, the air wet as a dog's tongue, and immense black-and-blue thunderclouds threatened on the horizon.

Sweet was at his desk, appreciating the air-conditioning, when the telephone on his desk jangled. He picked it up and heard the familiar automated voice informing him that he had a collect call from Jeffrey Sunnycalb. "Will you accept?"

"Yes," Sweet replied. "Hello, Jeff, what's up?"

"You need to find a girl by the name of Tiffany Ibarra," Sunnycalb replied.

"Why?"

"Because Penton kidnapped her and then let her go. … He said the girl's father asked him to do it to scare her. …"

"What?"

"… yeah, so she'd be scared of strangers. I asked

him why he didn't kill her, and he said, 'She was too damn cute to kill.'"

Sweet didn't know what to think. He'd check it out, but he didn't believe the part about the girl's father wanting to frighten his child by recruiting Penton. And why would a clever, cold-blooded killer like Penton let a victim, and potential witness, go because she was "too cute" to kill?

Still, he was always talking to Sunnycalb about the need to establish his credibility, and obviously the informant believed that this would help. If the story was true, Tiffany Ibarra could help break the case open; it would place Penton in Dallas abducting little girls, and a living victim might be able to identify him. Tiffany Ibarra wasn't in any of the files Sweet had seen, nor had her name ever appeared in the media as far as his research had uncovered. This was new information that might corroborate or expand on what was known about the cases. He also wondered if there could be more children who survived meeting Penton; if he let one go, maybe he'd done the same with others.

Trying not to let his excitement get the best of him, Sweet immediately began looking into Sunnycalb's latest revelation. He contacted the Dallas Police Department to see if there was an offense report from 1986 regarding a young girl named Tiffany Ibarra. They told him yes, such a report existed.

Sweet asked the Dallas PD to fax him a copy of the report. When he received it, one of Tiffany's statements immediately jumped out at him. She'd described the suspect's vehicle as a white van with brown trim. He'd seen such a van in a photograph taken of Penton's vehicle after his arrest for the murder of Nydra Ross.

He also noted that Tiffany's description of her

abductor closely matched Julia Diaz's description of the man who took Roxann. It was pretty generic, just an ordinary-looking, young white man with dark hair, and a thick, neat moustache, but coming from frightened little girls, the description helped establish a link between two living witnesses and two separate crimes.

Whatever tied one case to another was vitally important. It had long been assumed that the same vicious predator murdered Roxann Reyes, Christie Proctor, and Christi Meeks. They'd all been abducted within a ten-mile radius of Dallas, murdered, and their bodies dumped in another jurisdiction. After Mike Bradshaw dropped out of the investigation and Keith Grisham said he simply wasn't interested in Sunnycalb's claims, Sweet had taken it upon himself to familiarize himself as much as he could about all three cases so that when Sunnycalb, or anyone else, fed him some new piece of information, he'd know if it was corroborated by any of the other evidence. He didn't have the case files for Meeks and Proctor—they were still with their respective agencies—but he knew the basics.

Armed with these details, Sweet read Tiffany Ibarra's statement, given to police fourteen years earlier. He noticed when she described both important similarities *and* differences between the cases. One of the main differences he saw involved the suspect's vehicle, or vehicles.

In January 1985, two young boys claimed that Christi Meeks got into what they described as a small, gray or yellow car. In February 1986, according to the police report, Tiffany Ibarra told police that the man who grabbed her drove a white van with brown trim. Then a year and nine months later, Julia Diaz told the police in Garland that the man who carried off her friend, Roxann, drove a gray, four-door sedan. Four months after that, in March 1988, Penton raped and murdered Nydra Ross in a white van.

While the vehicle description wasn't the same for all four abductions, Sweet knew that fact could actually work in his favor. He believed that Penton had used two different vehicles—the van and the sedan. It was a fact that Penton drove a white van when he killed Nydra Ross. And one of the items in the chaotic mess of the Reyes case files was a title made out to David Penton for a gray, four-door Datsun sedan.

Sweet put the Ibarra case report down. He had no more doubts that that Penton was who Sunnycalb said he was: the incarnation of evil, a bogeyman who'd murdered at least five children, including his infant son, over a period of three years. He was in prison now, but these cases weren't just about making sure Penton stayed in prison the rest of his life, or even received a death sentence for his crimes.

Sweet's quest wasn't even all about Penton. The detective believed that every family of an abducted child deserved to know the truth. That the bogeyman who'd struck with such suddenness and seeming impunity had been identified and was paying for his crimes; that he would never harm another child or devastate another family. And, if possible, the families deserved the remains to be given back to them for a decent burial.

To remind him of what this was really about, and the reason he needed to keep pushing on whenever he felt overwhelmed or discouraged, Sweet gathered several photographs of Roxann, as well as news clippings, crime scene photographs, the incident report, and the composite drawing of the kidnapper. Then he created a small scrapbook, but not for any legal reason, not something to refer to in court or use to track his investigation. He called it his "inspiration book," and every time he needed to, he'd look at one of the photographs of the pretty child with the dark brown eyes, especially the one of her kissing her father, and push on. And if that wasn't enough, he'd stop and pray for strength and guidance.

Wherever the path was leading, Sweet knew he needed to find Tiffany Ibarra. So once again, he turned to LexisNexis, which had pioneered computer-assisted records searches long before there was such a thing as the internet and search engines. It was a shot in the dark. As with Julia Diaz, he had no idea if she was married and living under a different last name. Or for that matter, if she was still alive and would remember an event with any sort of recall that could help his case, even an experience as frightening as being pulled off the sidewalk by a stranger.

This time, LexisNexis turned up several Tiffany Ibarras. However, there was only one approximately the correct age. According to the computer program, she was living in Bay of St. Louis, Mississippi, about five hundred and fifty miles away. The computer report didn't contain a telephone number so he went back to old-school detective work and called the local sheriff in Bay of St. Louis.

As it turned out, Tiffany and her family were known to the sheriff, and in a Mississippi Delta accent thick enough to butter cornbread, the lawman said he'd be happy to help. In fact, he said he'd drive out to their place and, if she was around, ask Tiffany to give Sweet a call.

Hanging up, Sweet knew that the only thing he could do now was sweat it out and hope that he'd found the right Tiffany Ibarra.

CHAPTER TWELVE

August 16, 2000

As he was waiting to hear from Tiffany Ibarra, Sweet got another call from Sunnycalb that would prove to be one of the most significant of their relationship. The informant said the detective might be interested in a certain photo album that Penton kept in his cell.

In it, Sunnycalb said, were several photographs of young girls. And on the back of each photograph, Penton had written one of three letters: V, O, and A. "It's the code he uses to describe what kind of sex he had with them: V for vaginal; O for oral; A for anal."

Sickened by the thought of what the letters meant to the children, Sweet was also excited from an investigation point of view because it confirmed, and would to any jury, that Penton was a serial pedophile. But he didn't want to give Sunnycalb anything to let him know what he was thinking and kept his voice nonchalant as he asked, "What else?"

"There's pictures of cars."

Sweet furrowed his brow and thought about what the man on the other end of the conversation had just said. Sometimes Sunnycalb asked questions that made him think that the inmate was fishing for information, rather than trying to give it. And some of his questions were about the types of cars used by the suspect in the abductions of Meeks, Proctor, and Reyes. It was the sort of information a clever inmate might turn around and tell some other detective as if it was something incriminating the suspect had said, hoping to curry favor or make himself look more credible.

Although it wasn't easy, never forgetting that the informant was a pedophile, Sweet was always friendly when speaking to Sunnycalb. But he was also careful never to feed him any details or respond in a way that would give Sunnycalb, a master at playing off other people's reactions, a clue as to what he was thinking. But now Sunnycalb was volunteering information about cars in Penton's photo album that, if true, could provide another piece of the puzzle by linking photographs in the album to what he knew about the cars driven by his suspect.

As soon as he hung up with Sunnycalb, Sweet called the Warren Correctional Facility in Lebanon, Ohio, and asked to speak to someone who could tell him what he'd need in the way of a court order or warrant to seize an inmate's photo album. He was put in touch with prison investigator Shea Harris.

"That's easy," Harris responded. "I don't know what it's like in Texas, but in Ohio inmates have no right to expect privacy. Which inmate are we talking about?"

Sweet barely got the words "David Penton" out before Harris laughed. "It just so happens I have Penton's photo album sitting on my desk," the investigator said.

Harris explained that it was common practice to keep a close eye on inmates in the protective custody unit. "We want to make sure they're not smuggling in child porn."

"Are there any photographs of young girls in Penton's album?" Sweet asked.

"Yes," Harris responded.

"Do me a favor and look on the back. Is anything written?" Sweet asked.

After a moment, Harris said, "Yeah, there are some letters: V, O, and A."

Sweet nodded. Sunnycalb's credibility was getting better by the minute. "What about photographs of cars?"

Again, Harris confirmed what Sunnycalb had reported. "There's a photograph of a white van and one of a gray, four-door Nissan or Datsun. ... I can't tell which. There's some writing on the back, 'Monrovia and car packed for trip to Texas.'"

At Sweet's request, Harris made color copies of the photographs and mailed them to Garland. Witnesses said that a gray, four-door sedan was used in the Reyes and possibly Meeks abductions; he had the vehicle title for just such a Datsun registered to Penton in the Reyes case files box. He wasn't sure what Monrovia meant, possibly someone's name, but the writing on the back of the photograph indicated that Penton was going to drive it to Texas.

More pieces of the puzzle had snapped into place with the photo album; then a few days later, Sweet's telephone rang. "Detective Sweet, Garland Police Department," he answered.

"Hi ... this is Tiffany," a young woman said.

Sitting up in his chair, Sweet asked her if she'd ever lived in the Dallas area.

"Yes," she said somewhat timidly.

Sweet quickly explained that he was investigating an old case and looking for a Tiffany Ibarra who'd been kidnapped all those years ago.

"That was me," she replied and, when asked, recounted her story for him.

They talked a few minutes more when Ibarra blurted out, "I'm only alive by the grace of God!"

"You were a very lucky girl," Sweet agreed.

"Yes, I was because he killed a girl from my school a couple of days later."

Sweet nearly fell out of his chair. "What? Tell me what you mean?"

"He kidnapped and killed a girl by the name of Christie Proctor from my school," she replied.

The detective felt his jaw drop. He'd had no idea that Ibarra and Proctor went to the same school. He picked up the Ibarra incident report, and that's when he saw it; not only were both girls abducted from the same area, the killer grabbed them both on Waterfall Lane. The same street! He felt stupid for having missed it. Then again, so apparently had all the investigators before him.

Tiffany paused and then asked a question that threw him for another loop. "Why are you doing this?"

Sweet was confused. "I'm trying to find out who killed these girls."

"But I thought you already knew who did it," Tiffany replied.

Sweet furrowed his brow. This wasn't making sense. "I don't understand," he said.

Tiffany explained that in 1998, a female detective named Martha Sanders from Dallas and a detective from Plano named Keith Grisham had traveled to Mississippi to talk to her about the abduction. They'd shown her a photo lineup, and she'd picked one of the photos as being that of her kidnapper. She never heard from them again and thought that they'd solved the case.

Like fog lifting under the heat of the sun, Sweet suddenly understood why two years earlier Tammy

Lopez had called the Garland Police Department saying that she'd heard there was something new about her daughter's case. *Christie's mom must have heard about Tiffany and called Tammy,* he thought.

"No, the case hasn't been cleared," Sweet said. "Do you think you can remember what the man who kidnapped you looked like?"

There was no hesitation. "I can remember him like it happened yesterday," she replied. "I still see him in my dreams."

CHAPTER THIRTEEN

October 2000

After talking to Tiffany, Sweet felt like the case was coming together. Julia Diaz had mentally blocked the killer's face from her mind, but Tiffany Ibarra was telling him that she could positively identify him. If she could pick Penton out of a lineup and put him in the area where Christie Proctor was abducted, it was a big plus. It would take more than that, but he knew the case would take a big jump forward.

However, before he could meet with her, "The Job" got in the way and new crimes took precedence over old murders. There was no way around it, but it worried him. Delays, even necessary delays, can throw a wrench into the machinery of working a cold case. There's already been a long interval between the crime and the renewed investigation, with all the issues that can bring—evidence gets lost, witnesses disappear or die, memories grow hazy, people stop caring. Shelve the investigation again, and old leads that may have had some life breathed into them go back on the shelf.

Still, no matter what case he was required to work on, Sweet kept the injustice of what had happened to three little Texas girls in his mind. He accepted Sunnycalb's collect calls almost daily, even when the inmate had nothing new to report and just wanted to talk. They'd built a good rapport and he didn't want to mess it up by distancing himself from the informant. And when he really needed a reminder, he turned to the "inspiration book" on his desk.

Working murder cases over the years, he'd learned to disassociate himself from the person and focus on the crime and crime scene. It was the only way to keep his sanity. That was hard to do after talking to a victim's family and seeing the deceased as a person who was loved. But while it might sound insensitive to some, that was the way most homicide investigators survived over time.

However, for some reason, Sweet couldn't do that with Roxann Reyes. Most of the time when he picked up the inspiration book, he'd just look at the photographs of her and only see a little girl, not a body. But in this instance, he believed that staying emotionally involved helped him. Any time he got frustrated with the case, or was thinking that it was getting too difficult to deal with emotionally, he'd look at a photograph of her and consider what she must have been going through when she was with Penton. Was she crying out for her mother and father when he was hurting her? Then he would put aside the frustration and the darkness, and grow even more determined to make her killer pay for what he'd done.

However, that was easier said than accomplished. Penton had a long history of slipping through the cracks. Who knew how many times before he finally came to the attention of law enforcement he'd carried out his monstrous crimes, but investigators hadn't put two and two together, or missed some clue?

Certainly between the killer's first victim and his last, opportunities were missed to stop Penton. One chance was lost when the judge in Fort Hood let him out on an appeals bond after he pleaded guilty to manslaughter in the death of his son. It wasn't to say that a sentence for manslaughter would have put Penton away for life. In fact, he would have been out again while still relatively young, just as evil and just as dangerous; sexual serial killers get caught, or they die, but they don't stop for any other reasons. Yet, a prison sentence would have saved Christi Meeks, Christie Proctor, Roxann Reyes, Nydra Ross, and God only knew how many others in those years between 1985 and 1988.

In the meantime, a lot could have happened personally to Penton. He certainly would have boasted in prison about other crimes, as he liked to do now. Another inmate might have reported him, as Sunnycalb was doing now, and Penton could have been convicted on that evidence and given a longer sentence. Prisons are also dangerous places, especially for child rapists and murderers, the lowest of the low in inmate hierarchy; he might not have survived.

A break in one of the Texas cases early on might have also saved lives. Even before his arrest for the murder of Nydra Ross, Ohio and Texas law enforcement were communicating about his possible involvement in the Texas murders. But nothing had come of it, and even though he'd immediately become a suspect in the Ross case, he'd remained at large for almost another two years after the girl's disappearance.

Sweet didn't know why detectives in Texas didn't look harder at Penton. What he'd seen in the Roxann Reyes file, even as an inexperienced detective in 1996, made it seem that Penton was a strong suspect. Then he'd talked to Sheasby, the detective in Columbus who'd worked the Nydra Ross case, and he said he'd always believed that Penton was a serial killer and was responsible for the Texas murders.

Tiffany Ibarra's statements had surprised Sweet on several levels. The first had been the revelation that she'd already picked a suspect from a photo lineup for Grisham. But he also hadn't realized that Christie Proctor and Tiffany were abducted from the same street in Dallas. Grisham was with the Plano Police Department, and therefore Sweet had assumed Christie was from Plano; without the Proctor or Meeks case files, he'd missed those details.

Sweet called Grisham, who told him that Tiffany Ibarra's story was essentially correct. Sunnycalb had written a letter to the Plano Police Department about Penton's claim to have kidnapped Ibarra and set her free. He and Dallas police detective Martha Sanders then contacted Tiffany and she told them her account. But then Grisham interviewed Sunnycalb at the prison and decided that the inmate was an untrustworthy liar.

Even so, Grisham said, he'd presented his case against Penton, which included the Ibarra interview, to the Collin County District Attorney's Office. However, the assistant district attorney assigned to review the case concluded that the evidence only warranted a kidnapping charge, and even then, it wasn't a very strong case because he let the victim go. Nor, according to the ADA's assessment, did it prove he was involved in the murder of Christie Proctor. So the case was dropped.

By October, Sweet was beginning to feel overwhelmed by the Penton investigation. In addition to staying up with his regular case load, Sunnycalb kept feeding him information about all three Dallas-area cases. But without the other case files, he couldn't check what the informant told him against the details of the cases. He decided he needed help.

So one day Sweet jumped in his car and drove to the Mesquite Police Department planning to talk to Det. Mike Bradshaw about Sunnycalb, and tell him what he'd learned independently from Tiffany Ibarra, Penton's photo album, and the interview with Penton's sister. He thought some of it might be interesting enough to get Bradshaw to assist with the investigation.

Sweet knew from their earlier conversations that the Meeks investigation had been stymied by a couple of issues. One was that Bradshaw couldn't put Penton in the Dallas area at the time Christi Meeks disappeared or in Oklahoma, where her body was found. But Tiffany Ibarra put him in Dallas. And Sweet had learned from his conversation with Penton's sister, and her interview with the Ohio detective, Doberneck, that she and her husband had moved to Waynoka, Oklahoma, to avoid her brother having contact with their children. She'd later denied making derogatory statements about her brother, but she did admit that he'd visited her several times in Waynoka, which was about three hundred miles from Lake Texoma.

When he arrived at the Mesquite Police Department, Sweet was told that Mike Bradshaw had been transferred to Internal Affairs and that the new sergeant of the Crimes Against Persons Division was Bruce Bradshaw, no relation. So he asked to talk to Bruce Bradshaw. Following introductions, he was pleased that not only was the sergeant interested in what he had to say, Bradshaw and his former partner, Bob Holleman, had been assigned to the case the day Christi Meeks disappeared.

As Sweet quickly learned, it had haunted them ever since.

CHAPTER FOURTEEN

The past ...

In the year following Christi Meeks' disappearance, the two Mesquite detectives spent thousands of hours running down leads. They were both determined to find the killer, though their efforts often felt as if they were chasing their own tails. Then the nightmare was repeated ... twice.

In February 1986, Christie Proctor was abducted in Dallas, followed by Roxann Reyes' kidnapping from Garland in November 1987. Bruce said he and Holleman were soon meeting with detectives in the other jurisdictions to discuss similarities in the abductions, and then, when the other girls' bodies were discovered, their murders. They were all convinced that a single killer had been stalking the Dallas area, but although they tracked down several potential suspects, none of them checked out.

In 1988, Bradshaw said, he received a call from Det. Sheasby in Columbus, who'd been contacted by the grandparents of Roxann Reyes, which had, in turn, led to a possible suspect in the three Texas cases. His name was David Penton, who Sheasby believed was responsible for the abduction and murder of a girl named Nydra Ross in Columbus. Sheasby filled him in on the Ohio case and what they'd learned about Penton, including the murder of his infant son. The Ohio detective said he thought Penton was good for the Dallas-area cases and was adamant that he believed Penton was a serial killer.

Holleman was undergoing medical treatment for a thyroid problem at the time, so it was left to Bradshaw to follow up on the information. He spoke to the detective in Garland who was looking into Roxann's murder and subpoenaed Penton's military and criminal history. He then drove to Fort Hood and talked to Penton's second wife, Kyong, who was still working on the base, but she didn't tell him anything that helped.

Bradshaw told Sweet that he also thought Penton was a good suspect but wasn't able to connect him to the Dallas area or Oklahoma during the time of the Texas abductions. Without that connection, he and Holleman couldn't justify the expense to travel to Ohio to talk to Penton.

In 1991, Penton was convicted of the murder of Nydra Ross and sentenced to life in prison with the possibility of parole, but the three Texas cases went unresolved. However, it didn't mean that Bradshaw or Holleman ever forgot Christi Meeks. Suspects and leads would come and go; some looked promising, and many hours were spent investigating them, only to end in disappointment. Sometimes embittered ex-wives would call and point to their former husbands as good suspects, only for the detectives to find out their motives were revenge, not the truth.

Working child sexual assault cases, many times they came across suspects they thought might fit the profile of Christi's kidnapper and dared to hope that at long last, they'd found their man. One in particular, Paul Harvey Andrews, made them wonder if he was the bogeyman who'd carried off Christi Meeks.

Andrews had been convicted of rape in the 1970s,

sent to prison, and then was paroled back to Dallas County. In June 1985, he was identified as a suspect in another child sexual assault case that occurred not far from where Christi was abducted. The victim was twelve years old when she was attacked at a park in Mesquite.

They learned that Andrews was living in Garland, and detectives from Garland and Mesquite watched him for several days, thinking he would attempt to commit another crime. They seemed to be on to something, as he drove around elementary schools in Garland and stopped in shopping center parking lots, where he just sat in his car.

The young victim in the park case was able to identify Andrews from a photo lineup, and he owned a motorcycle similar to what she'd described her assailant driving that day. When Bradshaw and Holleman went to arrest him, Andrews met them at the door. *"I've been expecting you,"* he said.

Before they got him back to the police station, he confessed to the sexual assault in Mesquite. But even though they then questioned him for several hours, trying to link him to Christi's death, he denied responsibility. They even took him to the apartment complex where Christi was abducted to gauge his reaction, but he just shrugged and said he didn't recognize the place. The detectives finally had him polygraphed, and he passed.

Andrews' arrest didn't lead them to Christi Meeks' murderer, but they did learn from it. When he confessed to the sexual assault, Andrews explained that while he was driving around the schools and stopping in the parking lots, he was watching children and masturbating. Listening to him talk about how he targeted children helped the detectives understand the thinking of the sort of person who would abduct a child and then rape and murder her.

The investigation took its psychological toll on the detectives and their families. Bruce Bradshaw often thought about what had happened and the terror Christi must have been put through by the monster who took her. He would watch his children playing and enjoying life in all their sweet innocence, and think about the joy they brought to him and Gail. And yet that would remind him that the killer stole the joy of watching Christi play and grow from her parents.

As a police officer, Bradshaw viewed his job as a battle between good and evil, and in no instance was that more clear than the search to find Christi Meeks' killer. And yet, as the years passed and justice for Christi eluded him and his partner, it seemed that evil had triumphed. He became very distrusting of other people and avoided contact with the outside world, except his family, close friends, and fellow officers. He spent a lot of time trying to learn all he could about the sort of person who would commit such a crime and came to view the world cynically. Maybe he was just more conscious of it, but it seemed like a lot of kids disappeared during those years in Texas.

It affected his family, too, but not always in the way he and his wife could have foreseen. Jodi and Laci were very young when Christi disappeared. As they grew older, they became more aware of the time their dad spent trying to find the evil man who had taken her. They didn't question why he spent so much time away, or why he missed one of their school functions; they knew. He could tell it affected his daughters; they were very wary of strangers and developed the skill of reading people much the same way as a criminal investigator. Many times after meeting someone, they'd say something to the affect of *"that guy's a pervert."*

About a year after Christi's murder, Gail said to her husband, "Christi Meeks came to live with our family on January 19, 1985, and she never left." At times, it wore on her, avoiding the never-ending questions from family and friends. She'd never believed in sharing her worries and problems with others, except for her husband; sharing only made her issues theirs, too. She'd kept to herself the loneliness of losing so much of Bruce to his job, especially the Meeks investigation; even when he was physically at home, his thoughts and emotions would be focused elsewhere, as he tried to piece together the horrible puzzle. She became aware that there was a large part of Bruce's life, the heart of the Meeks case, that she couldn't be a part of, or share the burden of, until it was over.

She also bottled up her own fears that came from knowing some of what happened to Christi and dealing with the evil and darkness that had invaded her home when the child disappeared. She couldn't tell her friends or her family; she couldn't pass that evil on to someone else.

Yet, they found a way to get through it. Their Christian faith held the family together and protected them from the darkness. They learned to live with the ghost of a child in their home and move forward. She and Bruce even learned from Christi. They raised their girls to have faith, to enjoy living. Life, family, friends were all good things, but also be aware that evil existed in the world and guard against it.

A few years after Christi's abduction, their girls learned firsthand about evil when darkness once again threatened their family. Bruce and Gail were away, attending the State Fair. The girls were in Dallas, visiting her mom, who took the girls to a local ice cream shop. While enjoying their time with their grandmother, two armed men entered the shop, forcing everyone at gunpoint to lie on the floor while they robbed the registers. Bad enough almost turned worse when the robbers threatened to shoot a man and his wife, who were lying next to Jodi and Laci.

The robbers left without shooting, but Bruce and Gail heard the story that night; when they went to pick up the girls, they were met at the front door by Gail's mom and their daughters, talking all at once about their frightening experience. When they got home, the girls asked if they could sleep on the floor of their parents' bedroom. So Bruce and Gail made up beds and then listened while Jodi and Laci repeated their story over and over again. Talking seemed to relieve the fear, and finally they were able to fall asleep, secure in the knowledge that their parents were nearby, which was more than their parents were able to do.

The robbery reminded the Bradshaws of the delicate balance between life and death. Living with Christi and a trip to the ice cream store with a much-loved grandmother that could have ended horribly taught them to cherish family. The two tragic events actually brought them together and made them the strong, close-knit family they'd become. However, a darkness had entered all of their lives, and it would be many years before they could give it a name or chase it from their nightmares.

The lack of resolution in the case, however, was even tougher on Bob Holleman and his family. He was fixated on finding Christi's killer, and up until the day he retired, he would call Bradshaw at home to talk about the case or ask him to go along to chase down a lead. As long as he had something to do that might solve the case, he was energized and sharp. He told Molly that as long as he stayed busy, he didn't hurt.

However, when a lead came to nothing he'd sink down again, only lower. The officer who'd never missed a day now sometimes couldn't get out of bed or stop crying. Molly believed it was because of the immense guilt he felt because not only had he not returned Christi safely home to her parents, he couldn't even tell them who killed her. She knew these feelings were exacerbated when he'd come home and see his own children safe. He'd hug them and weep.

Then another tragedy compounded the torment Holleman was going through. About two years after Christi's murder, he was called to a crisis situation as the department's hostage negotiator. A distraught 16-year-old had locked herself into a bathroom at her parent's home with a gun. Holleman stood on one side of the bathroom door and talked to her for several hours, trying to convince her that she had everything to live for. He later told Molly that he thought he had talked her out of killing herself when there was a moment of silence from the other side of the door, and then the sound of a gunshot. As he stood there in shock and horror, a pool of blood crept from beneath the door.

When he got home that night, he kept telling Molly, *"I lost another one."* He didn't have to explain what he meant.

It seemed like every time he turned around, Molly's husband was absorbing another punch. When Christie Proctor and then Roxann Reyes disappeared, and it became apparent that a single killer was on the loose, he took it personally. He believed he should have caught the guy after Christi's abduction and was ravaged by guilt that two more little girls were dead because he didn't.

Worse, he told Molly that they had a viable suspect, but couldn't make a case against him.

Molly was losing her husband, and her children, including Michael, who was born in 1987, were losing their father. A month after Christi's body was found, he showed up for Emily's first birthday party, but was gone again as soon as it was over. Yet, he worried to the point of paranoia about their safety. At first he didn't want them to go outside in the front yard without an adult; then he demanded that they be watched in the backyard, despite a tall, locked security fence. Finally, he bought a large dog to guard them.

Making matters worse, Bob became addicted to the painkiller hydrocodone, a habit that began when he needed dental work and continued afterward. He explained to Molly, "It keeps me from hurting. I don't want to hurt anymore."

After the teen's suicide, Bob asked to be transferred out of the juvenile division and back to radio patrol. Some of that was for Molly's sake. It wasn't just the long, unpredictable hours, but also the physical and mental toll from his pursuit of Christi's killer, along with his normal caseload and work as the hostage negotiator. She longed for some sense of normalcy in the family, and regular hours were a place to start.

Bob was looking forward to it for a different reason. He told her that he knew that he would stay busy for eight hours, every shift, and busy was what helped keep the darkness away. For a time, it seemed to work. But within a year, he was transferred into the narcotics unit, and with that the new normalcy went out the window. He worked day and night trying to catch drug dealers, confiscating their cars and seizing their money and drugs.

There were benefits to the new job. He stopped taking hydrocodone and seemed happier than he'd been since January 19, 1985. Friends and family noticed. He made sergeant while in the narcotics division and led a successful team "crushing crime" throughout the Dallas area.

Still, Christi Meeks continued to haunt him. As he'd explain it to Molly, what did he care if some dope dealer got away with his crimes, he or some other cop would get him eventually. "It doesn't bother me that some guy sells a bag of marijuana," he said. "What bothers me is a guy who kills kids."

If he was having a good day, all it would take is the sight of a little girl who reminded him of the dead child, or sometimes nothing but a memory, and he'd sink like a stone back into depression. If he and Molly went to a restaurant, his eyes would constantly scan the faces of other customers and staff, looking for someone who matched the artist's sketch of the killer. He even confessed that sometimes he would see a car similar to the description of the car the Meeks suspect was driving, and he'd follow it to see who got out and whether they were stalking children.

Years after the murder he was still looking at faces and following cars. He told his wife that he knew it was silly—the sketch was at best an approximate, and the killer, even if he lived in Texas, wouldn't look like that anymore or be driving the same car. But he couldn't help it, he said; he just wanted "that son of a bitch."

The positive effects of working in the narcotics unit wore off. By Christmas 1989, Molly noticed he was falling back into bouts of depression that were more severe and closer together. He was cynical about the world and the people in it. He was gloomy and withdrawn.

By the beginning of the year, his demons had returned with a vengeance brought on by the approach of the anniversary of Christi's abduction, the birthday of his own daughter, and a pair of tennis shoes his mother-in-law unwittingly bought for Emily. Pink Cabbage Patch Doll shoes.

Bob said he "hurt," and again started looking to hydrocodone to numb the pain. Then he started talking about suicide, until one night he confronted Molly with a gun in his hand. She had Michael on her hip as he told her he was going to kill himself and wanted her to watch. Instead, she turned and left the room, shutting the door behind her. She took another step and then there was the sound of a shot. But he'd only done it to make her think he'd killed himself.

Molly didn't know what to do. He had tried psychiatrists and counseling, but it wasn't helping. She couldn't take it anymore, and they separated soon after he threatened to make her watch him shoot himself.

Even after that, the abduction and murder of Christi Meeks continued to insert itself into her life, that of her children, and especially her estranged husband. It permeated everything Bob did, even his time with his children. When Emily and Michael came home from visiting their father on the fourth anniversary of Christi's abduction, her daughter said they'd gone for a picnic, and then he'd taken them to the cemetery to put flowers on Christi's grave.

When Molly questioned Bob about it, he told her he'd been going to the cemetery on the anniversary every year. He explained that killers had been known to visit the graves of their victims at such times. In fact, the first year he and Bradshaw had even set a microphone in some flowers at the gravestone in case the killer dropped by to say something to his victim. No one had shown, but Bob had returned every year since, too, hoping that someday he'd see the man from the artist's sketch lurking there.

While other cops, like his partner, Bradshaw, and his supervisor, Lt. Larry Sprague, seemed to have the ability to put the case on a shelf when they came home, Bob couldn't. It might not have been the only factor in why they finally divorced in 1990, but The Call certainly was a major influence. Even Bob acknowledged that January 19, 1985, was the end of life as he knew it.

On the fifth anniversary of Christi's murder, Holleman, a gifted, thoughtful writer, wrote "A Letter to Christi's Killer," which was published in the January 1990 edition of *D Magazine*. He knew it was unlikely, he told Molly, but he hoped that somehow the monster who took Christi would see it.

> *"I think about you often, usually at the oddest moments—driving to the grocery, mowing the lawn, standing in line at the bank,"* he wrote. *"Your image unaccountably leaps to mind, produced by some randomly firing neuron in that section of my brain normally reserved for recurrent night terrors and childhood bogeymen. Since January 19, 1985, you have never been far from my mind. That day is indelibly etched in my psyche, as it must be in yours, but, of course, for different reasons.*
>
> *"Let me introduce myself. I am a policeman, maybe you saw me on TV, babbling to some earnest reporter about 'the incident.' ... Since 1985 I have moved on to different*

police assignments—three years investigating child sex crimes took an emotional toll that is frankly inexpressible. But there are some cases one never truly relinquishes."

After describing the events of the day that Christi disappeared, Holleman went on.

"The weeks and months that followed are forever embedded in my memory. You will pardon the cliché 'emotional roller coaster,' but I have no other adequate means of describing the false starts, dead-end leads, and blind alleys my colleagues and I encountered during that terrible time. And worn clichés do little to convey the anguish of parents simultaneously consumed with hope, horror, and dread.

"The taking of any human life is tragic. But it is different when a child is killed. I do not know if you understand tragedy in its truest sense: real, visceral tragedy. As yet having been spared the loss of loved ones, I must confess that I possessed only an academic comprehension of the term until January 1985, and the sense of tragedy I feel now is but a pallid approximation of that inflicted upon the parents of Christi Meeks. You have educated me about other extreme emotions as well. As you might reasonably expect, I have a considerable amount of hatred for you.

"While you do not know me, I do know a little about you: your approximate age, height, weight, and hair color. These mundane details recorded on a crime report form the basis of our acquaintance. They represent the raw material, the monochromatic details from

which we are expected to compose a completed portrait of you. In any police investigation the 'canvas' is added to by degrees. The bold brush strokes represent hard information gleaned from witnesses and physical evidence; the more subtle shadings are the result of experience in dealing with your kind.

"As you are doubtless aware, your portrait is presently far from finished, but

after several years of dealing with individuals who abuse, maim, and kill children, I have some inkling of your background. Laymen, repelled by the horror of these crimes, often have the mistaken impression that people like you bound fully grown from some wellspring of unfathomable evil. Some may even believe that an aberrant twisting of DNA doomed you to commit your offense. I can only speculate as to the horrors of your youth. Perhaps the atrocities you endured fomented a rage so profound that you were compelled to repeat them, to 'act them out,' as pop psychologists term it.

"It is easy to be seduced by pity for you, to want to see you only as a product of a disordered and abusive environment. This provides an explanation for your crime. And people desperately seek explanations for such horrific crimes. But an explanation, no matter how rational, does little to alter the brutal reality of your offense. I am deeply sorry for you. But do not expect forgiveness. Forgiveness implies a measure of understanding and mercy I am unable to muster.

"I often wonder how you feel, how you

exist. I know you must fear the late-night knock at your door. The consuming dread must tear at you. Do you sleep soundly? Or have you awakened at some early morning hour, sweat-drenched, heart pounding, because of a child's face thrust into your dreams? Do you remember? The face. That of a five-year-old girl.

"That face will reappear again and again, perhaps sometimes accompanied by another face as well—one you might not recognize, a visage vaguely defined and hazily indistinct. To suggest that your night terrors are caused by simple fear of capture does you an injustice; more sinister devils torture you. You have a conscience, albeit one stunted by abuse, and you know that you will be visited forever by an innocent, open, wondering face, and its avenging companion. Just as you are my nightmare, I am yours."

Holleman retired from the Mesquite Police Department in 1998 after twenty years of service. Addicted to the painkiller oxycodone and battling depression, he almost didn't make it that far.

The funny, kind gentleman Molly married, the brilliant, dedicated police officer who walked out of the door after The Call to look for a missing child, was himself missing. Shortly after their divorce, he called her and threatened her. "I'm coming over there, and when I get there, I'm going to blow your mother-fucking head off."

Holleman was arrested by his own department and charged with telephone harassment. He was told to attend anger management classes, which if he completed would result in the charge being dismissed. A class assignment was to write letters of apology to the people he'd wronged. One of the letters was to Molly, in which he took responsibility for their divorce. *"I am sorry for all the pain I have caused you over the past 4-5 years,"* he wrote. *"I often dream about life the way it was before drugs messed me up so badly ... like 1987 when Michael was born ... you, our home and our kids. ... I look back upon our years longingly."*

The letter was the beginning of the healing for Molly; it took some time, but she eventually forgave him. They became friends again, even after she remarried. Once upon a time, she'd fallen in love with him, and he was the father of her children. She decided she wasn't going to abandon him or push him away. She knew what lay at the heart of his troubles.

Others did, too. Holleman had always loved working for Lt. Sprague, and the feeling was mutual. Loud and occasionally crass, Sprague also had a heart of gold, and he made sure that whatever demons drove Bob Holleman, he was able to retire honorably with his pension.

In 1987, Bradshaw was also promoted to sergeant and transferred to the jail. The effect of the Meeks case on Holleman had been sad to watch; Bob had been one of the most intelligent and empathetic cops he'd ever known.

Bradshaw lost touch with his former partner when Holleman retired, but he didn't forget the Meeks case. Whenever a lead came in about Christi's murder, or a similar case would be in the news, the detective assigned to the case would come to him for the history or to run a name past him.

In 1993, he transferred from the jail to the Crimes Against Persons Division. Shortly after the transfer, one of the young detectives who worked for him attended a homicide investigation course put on by Lt. Vernon Geberth, a renowned New York Police Department homicide detective and author. The young detective brought back a placard with an inscription on it from Geberth's book that Bradshaw hung on the wall. It read: "Remember, we work for God."

To Bradshaw, it meant that no matter who suffered death at the hands of another and whatever the circumstances, the truth needed to be known. It didn't matter, he'd tell the detectives who worked for him, if the victim was a drug dealer or a little girl. No one deserved to be murdered or forgotten.

Any time tips came in about Christi's murder, he and his men would run them down until the leads were exhausted. He maintained a file on the case that took up several drawers in a filing cabinet. And always, always, he prayed that someday the person who kidnapped and killed Christi Meeks would be found and brought to justice. Then Gary Sweet decided to drop by the office and dredged up a name from the past that he recognized: David Elliot Penton.

CHAPTER FIFTEEN

November 8, 2000

Wearing casual shirts and jeans, the two detectives sat in the large open visiting room of the Warren Correctional Institute trying to look nonchalant. Sunnycalb had made it very clear; they were to dress and act as though they were just visitors, not detectives, or he wasn't going to meet with them. He wouldn't even see them in one of the prison's private interview rooms because, he said, the other inmates would find out and assume that he was talking to the police. He didn't want to be labeled a snitch.

Bradshaw had at first balked at Sunnycalb's demands, but he gave in when Sweet pointed out what happened to Plano detectives Grisham and Billy Meeks when he discovered the hidden camera. They either played ball by his rules, or they could lose their star witness. And it wasn't just Sunnycalb who might refuse to cooperate; two other inmates had come forward and agreed to be interviewed by the detectives, but they were taking their cues from Sunnycalb.

Sweet understood why Bradshaw and Holleman were haunted by the abduction and murder of Christi Meeks. The death of Roxanne Reyes had also been on his mind since the day he walked into the murder closet and looked in the two boxes of disorganized files that represented the extent of justice for a murdered child.

He was a family man, too, with his own daughters, and couldn't imagine the pain he'd feel if some beast like Penton hurt them. Sometimes he would think about how desperate the parents of Penton's victims must have felt when they couldn't find or help their children. He knew the case had affected his own children—that they had less freedom than some of their friends because he always wanted to be able to get to them if they needed him.

Other murder cases had come and gone, each with its own sad ending, each deserving of his efforts to find justice. Killers like Michael Giles committed their atrocities and, he'd helped put them behind bars. But the murder of Roxann Reyes and the other two little girls stuck with him like no others. And what made it worse was the thought of Penton sitting in his cell, "getting off" as he relived his depraved cruelty, and nobody holding him accountable for it. But he had more than he could handle alone and felt that partnering with Bruce Bradshaw, who'd been involved in the case from the beginning, was another example of divine intervention.

Sweet found a kindred spirit in Bradshaw. They were both devout Christians and devoted to finding a child killer. Sweet told him about Tiffany Ibarra and asked if he knew that Penton's sister, Amanda, had moved to Oklahoma and that her brother, David, had visited her there. *"She gave a statement to Columbus PD saying she was afraid when he'd visit and didn't want her kids around him. She also said she thought he killed the kids in Texas."* If true, it meant that Tiffany Ibarra could connect Penton to committing crimes in the Dallas area, and Penton's own sister said he'd visited her in Oklahoma.

Sweet showed him Amanda's statement and then

brought out the photographs from Penton's album that had been sent to him by Ohio prison investigator Shea Harris. One of the photographs showed Penton standing next to the gray, four-door Datsun, which matched the description of the suspect's car in the Reyes cases. He then handed Bradshaw the title to a Datsun four-door registered to David Penton. The car driven by the kidnapper in the Meeks case had been described as small and either yellow or gray.

Sweet was obviously excited about the information he'd put together, but Bradshaw was skeptical. He'd investigated numerous other suspects only to be disappointed in the end. Still, the new information put Penton in Oklahoma and possibly the Dallas area; they needed to check it out.

With Sweet present, Bradshaw had talked to Sprague, who was now the assistant chief at the Mesquite Police Department. Sprague was one of the best detectives Bradshaw had ever met, and he wanted his opinion on how to proceed. When Bradshaw and Sweet laid out the story and told Sprague that they wanted to travel to Ohio to talk to Sunnycalb in person, the supervisor didn't hesitate. "Go," he said and that's how they ended up sitting in a prison visiting room, waiting to talk to a pedophile.

Sweet had flown to Ohio the day before with another Garland police detective, Matt Myers, who was a native of Cleveland, which they thought might come in handy for getting around the state, but he'd also once worked for the juvenile division and had some insight on how pedophiles thought. Bradshaw and Don Phillips, a young Mesquite detective who Bradshaw had asked to help him with the Penton case, flew up the next day and met them at the prison. Sweet and Bradshaw would talk to the inmates while Myers and Phillips gathered records from prison investigators on the inmates they were interviewing.

One problem with pretending to be visitors was that Sunnycalb didn't know what they looked like and yet he was supposed to be acting like they were old friends. So Harris showed Sweet and Bradshaw where to sit, and then the informant was told where to find them so that he could pretend he knew them.

Having seen prison mugshots of Sunnycalb, Sweet recognized the paunchy, balding pedophile when he walked into the room. They all smiled and acted like best buddies who hadn't seen each other in awhile. Sunnycalb had threatened to hug them so that he could feel for recording devices, and Sweet had told him to go ahead. But the inmate apparently decided it wasn't necessary, and they all sat down after handshakes.

Sweet had been waiting for this moment since he'd first talked to the informant nearly four months earlier. So far, everything Sunnycalb said had checked out, and he'd recently passed yet another question about his credibility.

Detective Grisham had disparaged Sunnycalb's information, saying that the inmate's sister had filed Freedom of Information Act requests with the FBI and received some information about the cases as a result. Following up on the accusation, Sweet asked the FBI what Sunnycalb had seen. If the information he'd been giving Sweet was contained in the paperwork, it would destroy his trustworthiness. However, after looking at the records, it was clear that wherever Sunnycalb got his information, it wasn't from the records request. For one thing, there was nothing in the paperwork about the Roxann Reyes case; the FBI had declined to send

Christi Lynn Meeks was five years old when she was abducted from an apartment complex in Mesquite, Texas on Jan. 19, 1985.
Photo/Mesquite Police Department files

Several months after Christi's disappearance, 10-year-old witness Tiffany Easter, described this suspect for an artist's sketch.
Sketch by Bruce Greene for Mesquite Police Department

David Penton as he appeared in the spring of 1985 following his arrest for the murder of his 11-month-old son. He was released on an appeal bond and wasn't arrested again until 1990 during which time he killed at least four more children.
File photo

The body of Christi Meeks was discovered on April 3, 1985 by two fisherman floating in Deer Haven Cove, Lake Texoma about 75 miles from Mesquite, Texas, where she where she was abducted in January.
Photo/Mesquite Police Department

Life changed forever for Mesquite detective Bob Holleman and his wife, Molly, after he received "The Call" following Christi Meeks' disappearance on Jan. 19, 1985.
Photo/Molly Richarson

On February 12, 1986, Tiffany Ibarra was ten years old and walking to Bodie Elementary School in Dallas, Texas when she was abducted and then released by a young white man who had grabbed her on the sidewalk and pulled her into his van. She would be forever haunted by the bogeyman.
Photo/Dallas Police Department

Three days after Tiffany Ibarra's run-in with the bogeyman, Christie Proctor, a few days shy of her tenth birthday, was abducted while walking near Bodie Elementary School. Her remains would not be found for two years.
Photo/Dallas Police Department

After Christie Proctor's abduction, police detectives re-contacted Tiffany Ibarra who described the suspect for a police sketch artist.
Sketch/Dallas Police Department

Proctor's remains: Christie Proctor's skeletal remains were discovered beneath a mattress in a remote field near Plano, Texas in April 1988.
Photo/Plano Police Department

Shannon Sherrill was six years old in October 1986 when she disappeared while playing hide-and-seek in her mother's yard in Thorntown, Indiana. David Penton later told fellow inmates that he abducted and murdered her.
Media File Photo

Jeff Heck was a young Indiana State Patrol officer whose area included Thorntown, Indiana when Shannon Sherrill disappeared. Years later, he would contact Gary Sweet about David Penton's possible connection to Shannon's abduction. He concluded that Penton was the prime suspect and filed a report with the prosecutor's office in 2007 to that effect; the case remains "under investigation."
Photo/Jeff Heck

In 2003, a woman named Donna Walker (center) contacted Shannon's parents and claimed to be their long-lost daughter. Hoping for a "miracle" the parents' were taken in until Lt. Jeff Heck's investigation revealed that her claims were a hoax and arrested Walker.
AP Photo/Tom Strickland

Roxann Reyes was just three years old and picking flowers with her friend Julia Diaz in a field near an apartment complex managed by her mother when she was abducted Nov. 3, 1987.
Photo/Garland Police Department

Julia Diaz was ten years old when she narrowly escaped the man who then abducted her friend, Roxann. She described the killer for a police sketch artist; note the mole above the right eyebrow.
Sketch/Garland Police Department

David Penton after his arrest in April 1988 as a suspect in the abduction of Nydra Ross in Columbus, Ohio.
Photo/Columbus Police Department

Roxann Reyes' partial skeletal remains and her hair with a barrette still in it were discovered in a remote field near Murphy, Texas, in May 1988.
Photo/Garland Police Department

When Penton became a suspect in the disappearance of Nydra Ross, police seized his van and discovered traces of blood on the floor. The van also matched Tiffany Ibarra's description of the van her abductor was driving in 1986.
Photo/Columbus Police Department

Nine-year-old Nydra Ross was last seen alive talking to David Penton, a co-worker of her uncle who she was visiting in Columbus, Ohio in March 1988.
Photo/Columbus Police Department

Penton remained at large until 1990 when he was arrested for the murder of Nydra Ross. Convicted in 1991, he was sentenced to life in the Ohio State Penitentiary though would be eligible for parole.
Photo/Ohio Department of Corrections

Gary Sweet was a new detective with the Plano Police Department when he walked into the department's cold case "murder closet" and discovered the disorganized files for the Roxann Reyes case. It was the first step in a long journey.
Photo/Gary Sweet

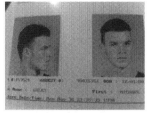

Part of Detective Sweet's learning curve investigating homicides was the murder of 80-year-old Smiley Johnson who was stabbed to death and sexually assaulted in 1996 by her grandson, Michael Giles, who was 15 at the time of the murder.
Photo/Garland Police Department

A fan of "death metal" bands and a satan-worshiper, Giles told Sweet that he sexually assaulted his grandmother because he wanted to experience necrophilia.
Journal/Garland Police Department

Satan worshipper Michael Giles was also the suspect in the brutal stabbing of a young black woman in the same neighborhood. However, despite the evidence, she claimed her assailant was an older black man.
Art/Garland Police Department

As Detective Sweet began to go through the evidence boxes in the Reyes case in 2000, he came across this photograph of the child with her father, Sergio Reyes, and was especially moved and determined to catch her killer.
Photo/Garland Police Department

As Gary Sweet got farther into the Reyes investigation, he kept an "inspiration book" with photographs of the child to remind him of who he was doing it for and combat the times when he wasn't sure he would succeed.
Photo/Gary Sweet

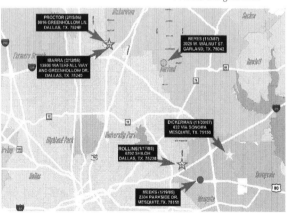

The bogeyman stalked his prey in the Dallas area during the mid-1980s, crossing jurisdictional lines to confuse law enforcement efforts to catch him.
Graphic/Garland Police Department

Gary Sweet (middle) and Don Phillips (right) talk to a Columbus PD detective outside of the house where Penton grew up and later lived as an adult. The investigators located twenty pieces of cloth tied together beneath the floorboards located in the attic. When tested the cloth revealed blood and semen stains; however, the stains were too old to give positive DNA results.
Photo/Garland Police Department

Albert Mulligan, a cellmate after Penton's arrest for the Nydra Ross murder, drew this picture of his daughter who'd died young ascending to heaven. He told Sweet that Penton had taken the drawing and put breasts on the girl then added the swing-set, merry-go-round and lake, which he said was in Texas.
Drawing/Garland Police Department

While detectives Sweet and Bradshaw talked to Penton at the Ohio State Penitentiary prior to his indictment, detectives Phillips and Meeks combed through Penton's tidy cell.
Photo/Garland Police Department

During their search, Phillips and Meeks discovered this plastic bag containing articles of civilian clothing tied together and hidden. They believe it was an "escape bag," put together by Penton should the opportunity to escape present itself.
Photo/Garland Police Department

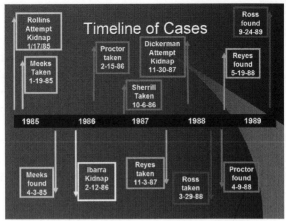

Detectives Billy Meeks and Don Phillips put together a Powerpoint presentation of the cases including this timeline that included two young women who stepped forward after Penton's indictment in the spring of 2003.

The Texas detectives involved in the Penton investigation following their interviews with Penton prior to his indictment for the Texas murders, from left: Bruce Bradshaw, Don Phillips, Marletta Scribner , Gary Sweet and Billy Meeks.
Photo/Garland Police Department

The Bogeyman as he appears now.
Photo/Ohio Department of Corrections

anything about it, stating it was still an "open case" and therefore not available. Why that same reasoning hadn't applied to the information given to Sunnycalb about the Meeks and Proctor cases, Sweet didn't know. However, even in those cases, witness names had been blacked out, and more importantly, there wasn't anything in the papers regarding Tiffany Ibarra. The information could have come from only one source: David Penton.

Sweet asked Sunnycalb during one of their daily telephone calls why he'd requested the information, and once again the informant gave him a logical answer. *"I'm sitting in this cell listening to him talk about killing these little girls, and I wanted to know if he was telling the truth."*

Still, Sweet and Bradshaw wanted to meet Sunnycalb face to face and judge for themselves whether they thought the informant was being honest. There were so many things to watch for in person that couldn't be done over the telephone, such as eye contact and body language. Most people's eyes dart away when they lie. And Sunnycalb would not be able to claim that some other inmate had just walked up if he suddenly stopped talking. No good detective would ever completely rely on an interview that wasn't conducted in person.

Over the next three hours, Sweet led the interrogation of the pedophile's recollection of what Penton had said, with Bradshaw filling in with questions about the Christi Meeks case. The conversation went well. They bought Sunnycalb a soda from one of the vending machines, and, despite the proximity of other inmates, he seemed to feel comfortable talking. The other inmates seemed focused on their own visitors, and the tables were far enough apart that it would have taken a real, and probably obvious, effort to listen to someone else's conversation.

In the end, Sweet believed that he was hearing the truth. The informant's body language and eye contact were good, and more significantly, his story stayed consistent and matched the evidence. Sweet was able to reconfirm what Sunnycalb knew about the Reyes case, plus there was one new bit of information. Sunnycalb said that Penton had told him that he originally planned to abduct Julia Diaz and settled for Roxann only after the older girl got away. That confirmed what Julia had told Sweet about Penton chasing her.

Sweet could also tell that Bradshaw was excited with what he was hearing about the Meeks case. Sunnycalb sold Bradshaw on his credibility when the detective asked if Penton ever described what was written on Christi Meeks' T-shirt.

"Color Me Rainbow," Sunnycalb said without hesitating.

Although the description of Christi's clothing had been made public when she disappeared, the amount of time between her abduction and Sunnycalb's statement indicated to Bradshaw that he'd heard it from someone else. And the most likely person was the killer.

The interview ended well. The detectives asked if he would take a lie detector test and he quickly agreed.

After Sunnycalb got up and walked out of the room, the detectives met in a private interview room with the first of the two new informants, David Korecky. Another pedophile, Korecky had been convicted of child molestation in 1986 in Sarasota, Florida. He was out of prison again when he was arrested and convicted in 1989 of molesting five children, boys and girls, aged 7 to 12, while baby-sitting and on camping trips working as a church youth counselor. He'd been sentenced to six one-year terms, but was again on the streets in 1994 when he raped two 10-year-old boys in Columbus, Ohio. He fled to Texas, where he kidnapped a young girl but was caught after leading police on a long chase.

A thin, nervous type of about 40, Korecky said he'd met Penton two years earlier. They'd both been in the Army, and that was their initial connection. However, it wasn't long before Penton began talking about raping and killing little girls. He'd started by savoring every detail of his attack on Nydra Ross. Then he'd moved on to talking about other murders in Texas, as well as Louisiana and Arkansas.

Penton also liked to boast about how smart he was, Korecky said, and how he'd carefully planned his atrocities by scouting out places to take the girls, where he could assault and murder them at his leisure and then dump the bodies. The killer was careful to cross jurisdictional lines after abducting his victims and then throwing them away like broken toys. That way he'd take advantage of the lack of communication between law enforcement agencies. "He likes to brag about how he'd beaten the system and had never been caught," Korecky said.

If that was true, Sweet asked, how did Penton explain that he'd been convicted of murdering Nydra Ross? He never admitted killing her, Korecky explained, and in Penton's warped mind, if he didn't admit it, the police didn't "get" him.

The detectives were soon convinced that Korecky was also telling the truth. One critical sign that seasoned investigators look for when they have multiple witnesses who could be colluding on their stories are differences in their individual accounts. If they're exactly the same, it raises a red flag that the stories are rehearsed. In fact,

Sweet and Bradshaw had talked about the possibility that Sunnycalb had coached the new informants to make himself appear more credible. However, that didn't appear to be the case with Korecky.

Calm and confident as he spoke, his recollections of what Penton had told him had enough small differences from Sunnycalb's accounts to ring true. He'd also described in at least as much detail where the bodies of Roxann Reyes and Christie Proctor had been dumped.

Still, it was the information he didn't have that made him more believable. He said he'd never heard of Christi Meeks. Even when pressed by Bradshaw, the informant didn't deviate from his contention that he didn't know anything about that case. If he was trying to impress the detective, he would have said what he thought Bradshaw wanted to hear. He, too, agreed to take a polygraph test.

After six hours of listening to two child molesters talk about the depredations of a different kind of monster, the detectives called it a day. They met up with detectives Myers and Phillips and then proceeded to a prison office, where they talked to Shea Harris. That's where the others filled Sweet and Bradshaw in on the details of the inmate informants' convictions.

The next morning, the detectives returned to the prison to talk to the third informant, another pedophile named William Wasmus. A former televangelist, Wasmus' arrest and subsequent conviction on seventeen counts of sex with minors, including raping a two-year-old boy, had been a big media story in Ohio. He'd been sentenced to 104 to 269 years in prison for his crimes.

Meek and mousy, Wasmus said Penton had talked about all three Texas murders. He said he'd met the killer three years earlier and immediately started hearing about the details of the killings. He repeated some of what they'd already heard from Sunnycalb and Korecky, with just enough differences and additions to be believable. But for some reason, Sweet found him to be "creepier" than the others.

Leaving the prison, the four detectives thought the trip had been a success, but there was a concern about what sort of witnesses they would make in court. All three had agreed to take lie-detector tests, but the tests weren't admissible in court. The men were believable, but they were also pedophiles, and there was no telling how a jury would react to testimony from child molesters.

Although finished at the prison, the investigators weren't done in Ohio. They drove to Columbus Police Department where they were given the Nydra Ross file to review. The similarities to their cases stood out clearly. When they finished with the file, the detectives had one more errand they wanted to accomplish before they went back to Texas. Sunnycalb had told Sweet that Penton once said that if he ever needed to hide something from the police, the best place was under the insulation in an attic. *"They'll never dig through the insulation,"* Sunnycalb quoted his former cellmate. So with the help of the Columbus Police Department, the Texans obtained a warrant to search his family's former home.

Penton's mother had moved out several years earlier, and another woman answered the door when the detectives dropped by. Sweet said that they were there to search the attic and explained why. "You go right ahead," she agreed.

Phillips, Myers, and Sweet went up into the attic while Bradshaw talked to the homeowner. Oddly enough, the woman's husband was in a back room watching television and never put in an appearance, even with three large men crawling around in his attic, pulling up the floorboards.

The woman told Bradshaw that she and her husband had heard rumors about David Penton and knew he'd lived there once. He decided to canvass the neighborhood to see if he could find anyone else who remembered the killer who'd lived among them.

At one point, the three detectives decided to take a break and came downstairs to find Bradshaw talking to a very pretty young woman and the older woman with her. During the conversation in the prison, Sunnycalb said that Penton told him that he'd lusted after a young Catholic school girl who lived on the same street as his mother's house. Bradshaw now introduced the visitors as that girl, now grown up, and her mother.

Both women said they thought Penton was "creepy" back then. "I told her," the older woman said, nodding towards her daughter, "to never be alone with him."

"She didn't have to," the younger woman added, "even as a kid I knew he was bad news."

The search of the attic took several hours. Finally, Phillips got down on his knees and reached under one of the floorboards. He pulled his hand back and held up what appeared to be just rags; however, they'd been neatly tied together with a piece of yarn that indicated there might be something inside. There wasn't, but they could see stains on the cloth and confiscated them. The rags were given to Bradshaw and Phillips, who were flying out the next day, to take to a DNA analysis laboratory in Dallas.

On the flight back to Dallas, Sweet looked out of the window as the brown fields and leafless trees of winter passed beneath and thought about the coincidences, or divine intervention, that had brought him to this point, faced with the task of making an evil child killer account for his crimes. What were the chances that the only detective in the Garland office the day Det. Diane Teft of the Fort Worth Police Department called would be the one who would recognize Penton's name? And why would he know the name? Because during a lunch break several years earlier, he'd wandered into the "murder closet" and discovered the Reyes case file gathering dust.

Who knew if another detective would have accepted Teft's invitation to question Sunnycalb? Or, if another detective would have realized that the informant knew details about the crimes contained in the files?

Yet, it wasn't another detective. It was Sweet who got the call. It was Sweet who stuck with it after others had given up. And it was Sweet who followed his gut instinct about Sunnycalb when others labeled the informant untrustworthy and a liar.

Now, it was Sweet who also could hear the plaintive voice of Roxann's mother asking if there was any news about the daughter she'd lost. As the jet touched down in Dallas, he was more convinced than ever that God had given him the task of making the bogeyman pay for what he'd done.

CHAPTER SIXTEEN

May 9, 2001

The first time Sweet talked to Roxann's mother, Tammy Lopez, he had to disappoint her by saying there was nothing new with the case. Almost three years after that telephone call and six months after returning from Ohio and his face-to-face meeting with Sunnycalb, he decided it was time to let her know that things had changed.

As usual, he'd been delayed by his current caseload. Within days of getting back from Ohio, he was assigned to investigate an officer-involved shooting that had quickly erupted into a media firestorm. Early on the morning in question, the 911 dispatcher at the Garland Police Department received a call that a fifteen-year-old black male was tearing up his parents' house after getting into an argument with his sister. The parents were gone; the youth was throwing belongings out onto the front yard and making threats.

When officers arrived on the scene, the young man, Justin Sanders, grabbed two large butcher knives. Bulling his way past the officer, D.S. Weands, the first responder to reach the front door, the teen ran outside. The officer followed Sanders at a safe distance, demanding that he put the knives down. The slow, foot pursuit circled the block and ended up back at its starting point, with Sanders declaring, "You might as well shoot me." That's when Weands shot and killed the youth, who, he said, had refused to drop the knives and had come at him.

The shooting immediately became sensationalized when the media picked up on the parents of Justin Sanders claiming that the shooting was unnecessary and racially motivated. It wasn't enough that Weands could be heard three times on a dispatcher's recording of the confrontation ordering the youth to drop the knives before he pulled the trigger. The media barrage aimed at the Garland Police Department portraying Sanders as an innocent teen and the officer as a trigger-happy killer lasted for several days. There were daily interviews with the family, who erected a huge sign in their yard stating: "The Garland Police Killed Justin Sanders."

Although they did not say so publicly, the Garland Police Department knew that Sanders was no angel. A week before the shooting, his own family had reported that he'd held a knife to another teen's throat, and he had a record for other crimes. However, that didn't excuse the officer if he'd shot him without cause, and Sweet, who'd been assigned as lead investigator, was busy assembling the evidence to be taken to a grand jury.

After three days of the media bashing his department, however, Garland Police Chief Larry Wilson called a press conference, at which time he showed the assembled reporters and photographers a video. As it turned out, one of the other responding officers had parked his vehicle in the middle of the street with its emergency lights on, which automatically starts the car's dashboard camera. The camera caught the action just as Sanders walked in front of the car and then turned and came at the officer, raising the knives. At a distance of only six feet, Weands fired a single shot that struck the youth in the chest, killing him; the teen had literally fallen with his head on the officer's shoe.

It was clear to Sweet that Weands had waited until the last second to defend himself, even ignored his training to do so. Police officers are taught that even at seven yards—three times the distance Sanders was when he turned on Weands—an assailant with a knife can close the space between them before an officer can stop him with a bullet.

When the Sanders family was shown the video by the media, they still insisted the shooting was unnecessary because the teen "didn't lunge" at the officer. Other armchair "experts" in the public opined that at that distance, the officer could have just "wounded" Sanders by shooting him in the arm or leg. Obviously they had no real world experience in the difficulty of hitting a small, moving target, which, even if successful, wouldn't necessarily stop an attack. But they, of course, all knew better.

However, the media understood what they were seeing and the criticisms aimed at the Garland Police Department went away. They'd just assumed that the police were in the wrong, but when shown the evidence, they changed their tune. There were no more interviews with the family. Sweet noted the irony that when the press saw that the shooting was justified, it simply wasn't a good story anymore.

The Sanders case was followed in December by the murder of Keith Calloway, a homosexual black male who had been hog-tied and had his throat cut several times. Investigating the case was an eye-opener for Sweet, who found himself spending a lot of time in gay bars interviewing possible witnesses. It was a slice of life he'd never been exposed to, but he knew that Calloway liked going to the clubs, and Sweet believed that he had been killed by someone he picked up. He hoped that someone might have seen him with the suspect.

As much as he tried to look at the investigation as "just the job," it was yet another murder that affected him personally. Meeting Calloway's mother and stepfather, who'd raised him from the time he was a baby, and his brother, he knew they loved the victim, and their grief made it tough to disassociate himself. He never found the killer, though he had good DNA evidence that he entered into the national database in the hope that someday there would be a match. But he promised Calloway's stepfather that he wouldn't quit looking for Keith's killer. Instead of the department's "murder closet," he kept the case file on his desk, next to Roxann's inspiration book.

In May, Sweet decided it was time to find Roxann's mother. He'd waited because he didn't want to get her hopes up until he felt like he really had something. In fact, he would have waited longer still, but he needed something from her.

DNA analysis of the stains on the bundle of rags taken from the attic of Penton's family home had revealed minute traces of blood, semen, saliva, and hair. The lab wanted genetic material from Roxann for comparison, but in 1988 DNA was virtually unknown, and the girl's remains had been buried. The next best thing, however, would be a sample taken from her mother.

Tracking her by her social security number, Sweet learned that Lopez was working at a nursing home in Kaufman, Texas, about forty miles south of Garland. He drove to the nursing home, but she wasn't there; however, the manager gave him her home address in Kemp, which was another ten miles to the southeast.

When he drove up to the single-wide trailer, Sweet

was stunned to see a young girl of six or seven playing in the front yard. She looked like how he would have imagined Roxann to look at the same age. He realized that he was looking at a sister who'd been born after Roxann was abducted.

Sweet hadn't called ahead, and Tammy Lopez seemed stunned when she answered the door and he introduced himself. He asked if she remembered calling him nearly three years earlier. She did, and then when he explained what was going on, she broke down and began to cry before inviting him into her home.

When she was able to pull herself together, Tammy said she was happy that someone was looking at the case again and seemed to be making progress. The rest of the world might have forgotten her little girl, but she had not. She lamented that she'd lost most of her photographs of Roxann in a fire and was grateful when Sweet said that there were several in the file at his office, including those he had in his inspiration book. "I'll make you copies," he promised.

They talked for a long time. As Lopez recalled the day her daughter disappeared, Sweet could tell that the abduction had changed her life, and not in a good way. She seemed … empty … and had obviously never recovered from the loss. However, she then surprised him by saying that she wasn't convinced that the remains of the child found in a wooded field near Murphy, Texas, belonged to her daughter.

"What do you think happened to her?" Sweet asked.

"I think her father had her kidnapped and taken to Mexico," Lopez replied.

Indecision troubled Sweet as he looked at the woman's distraught face. She'd sounded hopeful and obviously wanted to believe that her daughter was alive somewhere so badly that she couldn't accept the truth. She was a mother waiting for a miracle, and who was he to destroy that? But she couldn't be insulated from reality if and when Penton was brought to trial for Roxann's murder. She needed to accept the truth now, while she could deal with it away from a courtroom, away from the press. He shook his head and looked in her eyes as he quietly said, "No, she's dead, and her father didn't take her."

Still, she resisted. Sweet understood. She was no different than all those families of missing children who set a place in front of the empty chair at the dinner table, who left the light on every night as a beacon for the lost, who refused to put away the stuffed animals and toys, or take the posters down from the walls of a child's bedroom.

It didn't matter that there never had been much hope the day a stranger changed her life. In 1999, the National Center for Missing & Exploited Children released a report that every year 800,000 children were reported missing in the United States. Most, 97 percent, were taken by a parent, family member, or acquaintance, and 98 percent of those eventually returned home. The majority of those who didn't were believed to be runaways.

However, a little more than one hundred children very year were considered the victims of a "stereotypical kidnapping" by a stranger, and most of those ended tragically with the victim exploited by the child sex-trafficking industry, or sexually assaulted and murdered. In the cases in which the perpetrator intended to rape and kill the child, time was of the essence for law enforcement to intervene. A Washington state study concluded that in 76 percent of the murders of an abducted child, the victim was killed within three hours; in 89 percent of the cases, the victim was murdered within twenty-four hours. But tragically, in 60 percent of the cases, more than two hours passed between someone realizing a child was missing and the police being notified. And by then, it was almost always too late.

Although Sweet was aware that one child, Tiffany Ibarra, abducted by Penton had lived to tell the story, she was the only known survivor of an encounter with him. Little Roxann had not been so lucky; her remains had been found in a field and identified by law enforcement. But for fourteen years, her mother had waited for her to come home; she needed proof.

So Sweet offered to show her the video of the steps the crime lab used to identify her remains in an era before DNA testing. She said she wanted to see it, but she also wanted her mother to be with her, so they postponed the viewing until her mother and stepfather could drive down from Ohio to support her.

In July, Tammy, and her mom, Joyce, arrived at the Garland Police Department. Sweet and a crisis counselor escorted them to a conference room to view the video.

Fourteen years after her daughter broke down into a weeping mess when no kidnapper showed up at the airport with his hostage, Joyce Davis approached this meeting with both hope and trepidation. Hope because, according to her daughter, a detective was back working on the case, and trepidation because of what it might do to Tammy. Her tough, hard-working firstborn had never been the same after Roxann disappeared.

Joyce's husband, Paul Davis, was the one who'd pointed out the connection between Penton and Roxann's murder. In 1990, he'd been driving back to Minford from a job in Columbus, when he stopped to get gas and saw a somehow-familiar face of a man staring out at him from the front page of a Columbus newspaper. There, in black and white, was the spitting image of the sketch the police artist had drawn from Julia Diaz's description of Roxann's kidnapper. Only it was a photograph of David Penton, who the story said had been arrested for the murder of Nydra Ross and was a fugitive from Texas for shaking his son to death. Paul turned around and drove to the Columbus Police Department headquarters and told the detectives investigating the Ross murder about Roxann and pointed out the similarities between Penton's mugshot and the sketch.

That had been a long time ago, so long that Joyce had given up any hope that something would come of it. Every day, she looked at her photograph of Roxann and prayed for her. Now, she and Tammy were at the Garland Police Department talking to a detective, who had seen the Columbus newspaper articles and was connecting the dots back to her granddaughter's murder.

The crime destroyed Tammy's marriage to Sergio Reyes. Sometimes tragedies draw couples closer to deal with it together, but others are torn apart. The Reyes' heard the whispers from others, saw the letters to the editor of the newspaper blaming them for what happened, even suggesting that one and/or the other had something to do with it. But what they couldn't overcome was the blame they placed on each other, and that led to divorce.

Tammy had since remarried, and she and her husband, Jesus Lopez, had two children, a boy and the girl who made Sweet do a double-take when he saw her playing in the yard. However, Tammy had changed. She was no longer motivated to do anything with her life; she couldn't hold a job and didn't care. She cried a lot for her lost child.

After Roxann's remains were found scattered in the field where she'd been discarded, Tammy refused to accept them as her daughter's. Not even the long dark hair with the clip that Roxann had worn in it convinced her. At the funeral services, she wanted to open the casket containing her daughter's skeleton. *"That's not my baby in there,"* she'd insisted.

Tammy couldn't bear the thought of Roxann's murder. So she came up with a different theory: that her former husband, Sergio Reyes, had spirited their daughter back to Mexico and that she still lived; that someday there would be a joyous reunion.

Now, Det. Sweet was going to prove to her that the remains were Roxann's, and Joyce was worried about how her daughter would react. But if that's what it took to make this monster—this David Penton, if he was the guy—pay for what he did to Roxann, then Tammy was going to have to be brave and come to grips with the truth.

After everyone had settled into a seat, Sweet showed the video that had been taken of the examination of Roxann's remains. Some of the identification process was a visual inspection of the skeleton. Searchers found most of her bones, as well as her long dark hair with a hair clip still in place; the skull still had all of its teeth intact, revealing a distinctive space between the two top front teeth, which matched Roxann's dental history.

However, the main method of identification was through photo superimposition. Basically, the technique involved superimposing a photograph of the victim, in this case Roxann, over a photograph of the skull found in the field. By matching certain features of the skull with those on the photograph, an analyst could say whether it was a match to a high degree of certainty—enough certainty that the technique was widely accepted for identification in most courts in the world.

As they watched the video, Tammy Lopez and her mother both began to cry. It was difficult for Sweet to see, and he felt guilty knowing that he was destroying whatever hopes she had that her daughter was still alive. But he also believed that she needed to know the truth. He would have wanted to know if their positions were reversed, and she deserved that, too. And it could be important if Penton was brought to trial.

When the video finished, Tammy Lopez wiped her tears off her face and nodded to Sweet. "I believe you," she said, her voice hoarse and subdued.

"I don't understand why you weren't shown this video before," Sweet said.

Lopez shrugged. "I guess they were trying to spare my feelings."

"I don't agree with that philosophy," he replied. "I think you have the right to see anything involving your child. Is there anything else you'd like to see now?"

Tammy thought about it for a moment. "I'd like to see the composite drawing," she said. "I was in the room when it was done, and I want to see it again."

Sweet opened his "inspiration" notebook to the sketch of the suspect. Lopez reached over and touched the face above the right eye. "I remember the mole that Julia described."

The detective looked where she was pointing. He hadn't noticed the mole before, but he could see that the artist had, indeed, drawn one.

The only photograph he had of Penton was his booking mugshot from his 1989 arrest in Ohio; his hair covered his forehead in that picture. Sweet excused himself, and while Lopez talked to the crisis counselor, he ran to his computer and pulled up a more recent photograph taken of Penton from his Ohio prison record. Sure enough, a distinctive mole stood out above his right eyebrow.

Sweet called Bradshaw in Mesquite and told him about the mole. Bradshaw immediately recalled what Tiffany Easter had said about a mole on the suspect's cheek. She was only nine years old at the time and severely traumatized; it wouldn't have been unusual for her to remember the mole without recalling exactly where it had been on the suspect's face three months after the kidnapping. He looked in his files at the mugshots he had of Penton, but hair covered the area above his right eye. Then he called up the same photograph from the Ohio prison that Sweet was looking at, and sure enough, the mole stood out on the killer's face like the mark of Cain.

It was an important detail, and one that Sweet had almost missed. Once again, fate or divine providence had intervened so that Tammy Lopez wanted to see an old composite drawing and pointed out the mole. It was a distinctive physical characteristic that eyewitnesses, Julia Diaz and Tiffany Easter, had described, even if Easter had described the mole being on his cheek. After all, she'd been a frightened nine-year-old child.

Sweet would later track down the police artist who did the sketch from Julia's description. She, too, remembered the nine-year-old child's description of the man with the mole on his face. It was no accident she'd drawn it above his right eyebrow.

CHAPTER SEVENTEEN

June 2002

S weet couldn't believe his ears. Along with Bradshaw and polygraph operator Bill Parker, a retired police officer who was now in business for himself, he'd flown to Ohio to take final statements from Sunnycalb, Korecky, and Wasmus. The statements were necessary in case any of the informants were called to the witness stand and then reneged on what they'd said or changed their stories. But there was a hitch. Through his attorney, Sunnycalb had just presented a list of demands that he wanted met or, he said, he and the other two weren't going to cooperate.

Furious, Sweet would have kicked Sunnycalb's flabby ass right then and there if he could have gotten away with it. They were paying Parker a hundred and fifty dollars an hour, plus expenses, and Sweet was thinking about how he would now have to explain to his supervisors why all that money was spent and he had nothing to show for it.

There'd already been enough delays in pursuing the case. After showing Tammy Lopez the video imaging used to identify Roxann's remains and getting a DNA sample from her in July 2001, the detectives didn't receive a report from the DNA laboratory until February 2002. Even then, the results weren't what they'd hoped. The lab stated that the DNA material was so degraded that they could not match it to Meeks or Proctor; however, they could not rule out Roxann, though that wouldn't mean anything in court.

Although disappointed, Sweet still felt like they had enough of a case to charge Penton when he met that same month with Dallas assistant district attorney Jane Whitaker to discuss the case. Whitaker was what they called an "intake ADA," who was responsible for the initial assessment of a case before it was assigned to a prosecuting assistant district attorney to be taken before a grand jury. It was her job to review the evidence, make sure the detectives had crossed their t's and dotted their i's, and if necessary go back out and get more evidence. She was a matter-of-fact professional with a reputation for being tough but fair.

After Sweet talked about the cases, Whitaker agreed that there was probably enough evidence to go to the grand jury. But, she added, there was more work for the detectives to do before she'd recommend it; she wanted them to pull the cases apart so she could judge each on its separate merits.

So Sweet and the others went back to tie up loose ends, working together due to the intertwined nature of the investigation, but each handling the details associated with their respective cases: Sweet taking care of Reyes; Bradshaw and Phillips handling Meeks; and a newly invited member of the team, Plano police Det. Billy Meeks, to work the Proctor case.

Meeks, who'd joined the Plano department in 1980 and made detective five years after that, had off and on been part of the Proctor investigation since 1988, when her skeletal remains were discovered under a burned mattress. He'd helped process the crime scene, including the painstaking job of sifting the ground looking for bones and related evidence two years after her abduction near Dobie Elementary School.

Not long after that, he first heard the name David Penton, who'd just been arrested for the murder of Nydra Ross in Ohio. A Columbus police detective called the Plano PD about a possible connection between Penton and child murders in Texas. There were some differences between the Ohio case and Christie Proctor that didn't necessarily shout "serial killer"—the races of the victims and the circumstances around the abductions—but there were also similarities, such as crossing jurisdictional lines and depositing the bodies in remote, wooded creek beds.

However, the Plano investigators weren't able to put together a case on Penton at that time. Nor, for that matter, in later years, though several detectives had been assigned to the case and worked it when new information continued to drift in over the years. Although never specifically given the lead in the case, Meeks had gone as backup with Grisham to Ohio in the failed attempt to talk to Sunnycalb, and he'd even spoken briefly to Tiffany Ibarra when the other detective was trying to corroborate her story. Yet, there remained too many missing pieces.

Meeks was a great addition to the team. He'd grown up in the hard-knocks Dallas neighborhood of Pleasant Grove, where it seemed like the career choices were: cop or criminal. He was the kid who always wanted to be the police officer, whether it was playing cops and robbers with his buddies or when he dreamed of the future. As a detective, he prided himself on always trying to do his best and his work ethic.

The variety of his experience made him an asset to the Penton investigation. As a detective, he'd been assigned to a variety of units within the Plano detectives bureau—juvenile, property, narcotics, and crimes-against-persons as a homicide investigator. In 1997, he'd been asked to work with FBI and DEA task forces investigating drug-related deaths. With the feds, he'd learned how to integrate multiple agencies to share information and work as a cohesive unit, which helped when he got a call from Sweet and Bradshaw. They said they were looking into the murders of Christi Meeks and Roxann Reyes; they knew that the Christie Proctor case was thought to be connected and wanted to know if he'd consider joining forces. He jumped at the chance and invited them to meet with him in the Plano PD "war room," used for multi-media strategy sessions. Before they left Plano that day, they all had copies of each other's files, and a plan on how to proceed as a team.

Bradshaw and Phillips were particularly busy following up loose ends on the Christi Meeks case. They drove to Oklahoma, where Penton's now-former brother-in-law, Andrew, still lived. The man described to the detectives how on the way home from work with him, Penton always wanted to drive around schools looking at young girls and fantasizing about raping and then killing them. In particular, he said, they haunted Catholic schools and commented on the short uniform dresses. He said he thought it was all a dark fantasy but apparently more than that to Penton.

Bradshaw and Phillips also drove to Arkansas to talk to Penton's sister, Amanda. She confirmed that she and her ex-husband had been living in Oklahoma, near Waynoka, when Christi Meeks disappeared.

One of the trips taken by the Mesquite detectives only added to some of the confusion when they went to the Fort Hood-Killen area and spoke to Kyong. This time, Penton's second wife remembered that early in January 1985 she and her ex-husband purchased a Datsun sedan. Her husband had then disappeared for about two weeks; she assumed he'd gone to Fort Bliss in Louisiana to visit his friends.

The Mesquite detectives used the Vehicle Identification Number (VIN) from the title Sweet had in his possession and tried to trace the car. They eventually found it in Kentucky and asked an FBI forensics team to search it for evidence, such as old bloodstains. No evidence was located, but the FBI sent them a photograph of the car. Only it wasn't gray, it was brown with a yellow racing stripe along the side.

The discrepancy didn't rule out that the car had been repainted or that Penton had used a different car. The two young Hispanic boys who reported seeing Christi get in a car with a stranger were confused about the color, one saying it was gray and the other that it was yellow. Also, Kyong said Penton was a good mechanic and often worked on cars owned by his friends and neighbors, sometimes keeping the vehicles for a period of time to use.

The detectives never got around to pulling the cases apart for Whitaker. Instead, five more months passed between meeting with her and returning to Ohio to get official statements from the informants. And now after all the work they'd put into the investigation, including the time spent on the telephone in almost daily calls from Sunnycalb, the inmate wanted to play games.

Most of Sunnycalb's list was a bunch of penny-ante bullshit—small items he and his fellow informants wanted to make their lives more comfortable in prison—but they also wanted to be subpoenaed to Texas to testify before the grand jury. Sweet couldn't agree to any of it without talking to the prosecutors in Texas, but he wasn't even inclined to ask.

Since the day he started talking to Sunnycalb, Sweet had known that the informant's motivations weren't altruistic. Sunnycalb was looking out for Sunnycalb. All throughout their dealings, the informant wanted the detective to make telephone calls and write letters on his behalf to the judge and prosecutor from his case and let them know what a great help he'd been. He was clever about it, too, insisting that Sweet write and then send them to him so that he could read what he said before he mailed them.

Sweet didn't want to turn the informant down and have him decide not to cooperate, but neither did he want to help a twice-convicted pedophile get out of prison any time soon. So while he wrote the letters and gave them to Sunnycalb to read and mail, he also called the men and explained the circumstances. They laughed and thanked him for the explanation.

Now, looking at the list of demands Sunnycalb had made in exchange for his cooperation, Sweet shook his head. He tossed the list of demands back to the lawyer. "I'm not even going to ask."

Sunnycalb's attorney agreed with the detective and tried to reason with his client. But Sunnycalb was adamant: Meet his demands or he and his friends weren't talking.

With angry Texas lawmen sitting in his office, prison investigator Shea Harris wasn't taking Sunnycalb's extortion attempt lightly. He had the three inmates thrown in solitary confinement for hindering an investigation. But it didn't help Sweet with the issue of going back to his boss with empty hands.

Later, Sweet would come to look upon Sunnycalb's

recalcitrant behavior as another instance of divine intervention. But at the time, he tried to think of how to recover from the setback by asking Harris a simple question. "Can you think of any other former cellmates we can talk to?"

Harris thought about it for a moment and then nodded. He picked up the telephone and asked that an inmate named Tony Baker be brought to his office. Baker wasn't a pedophile or a sex offender; in fact, he was a simple burglar who'd run afoul of a prison gang and had been placed in the Protective Custody unit for his safety.

As soon as the detectives explained what they wanted, Baker agreed to talk. He didn't like Penton. In fact, Penton talked so much about raping and killing kids that he'd once grabbed the monster and shoved him up against a wall. "I told him I didn't want to hear any more."

Although he wasn't as detailed as some of the other inmates were—"I tried not to listen"—Baker did describe what Penton had told him about killing little girls in Texas and added that his former cellmate also discussed killing children in Arkansas and Louisiana. "He's obsessed with talking about it," he said.

Baker was a godsend. Not only was he verifying the same information the three convicts now cooling their heels in the hole had given, he hadn't come to the detectives with the information. No defense lawyer could say he was trying to make a deal or getting even with Penton for some grudge. Plus, a burglar would come off better in front of a jury than a pedophile.

The next day, their luck got even better when Harris called again. He'd remembered that prior to Sunnycalb, Penton had shared a cell with a former cop who had already assisted prison authorities with breaking up drug rings in the prison. The detectives drove back to the prison, this time to meet with Timothy Creighton.

A non-descript man in his fifties, Creighton was a decorated Vietnam War veteran and had worked for the Bethel, Ohio, police department. According to Harris, the story was that a friend asked Creighton to go with him to a drug house to get some money that was owed to him. Apparently, things went sideways; the friend ended up getting shot, the drug dealer was killed, and Creighton ended up with the money. He was then tried and convicted of murder.

Former police officers are always at risk in a prison environment, and so Creighton was placed in the Protective Custody Unit. That was when he was stuck in a cell with Penton.

When Sweet explained why he and his partners were at the prison, Creighton didn't seem the least bit surprised. "What took you so long?" he asked. "I've been wondering when someone would get around to asking me about Penton." He said that Penton talked about almost nothing else except raping and killing children. Even if the conversation started on another topic, he said, within a short time his former cellmate would turn it to his favorite horrific subject.

Creighton said he first met Penton when the other inmate approached and asked if he had been a cop. Apparently believing that the "convict code" was stronger than Creighton's ties to his former occupation, Penton told him that authorities suspected him of murders in Texas and Louisiana. He was worried that some evidence would come back to haunt him; in particular, he wanted to know how long DNA material, such as semen and blood, would remain on a victim's body.

"I told him it depended on how they'd been disposed," Creighton said. "He said he'd dumped some in the open and put others in water."

The former police officer said he'd followed old habits and taken notes of his conversations, however he was secretive about it. He'd just listen while Penton talked and then write down what he said when the killer left the cell. Creighton couldn't find his notes while the detectives were still in Ohio, but he said he would look for them.

Instead of being a waste of time and money, the trip to Ohio had produced two more good witnesses. And they might not have talked to them if Sunnycalb had cooperated.

Creighton eventually found his notes and mailed them to Sweet. One mentioned the Driftwood shopping center in Mesquite, where Penton said he would try and pick up young girls. This was important because Driftwood was an obscure, out-of-the-way mall and not a place Creighton would have likely pulled out of thin air.

The notes also referred to Penton visiting a young woman on a street in Garland called Treeline. Sweet looked up Treeline on a map and went there to look around. He was disappointed to see that it was a new neighborhood, built after Penton was arrested in Ohio.

Creighton's information seemed to be wrong. However, Sweet decided to call the prison and ask Harris to get the inmate on the telephone. The former police officer said that it was possible that he misheard Penton. But, he said, he believed that the street would have a name similar to Treeline.

Sweet hung up and again went to check out a map.

Roxann had been abducted from Walnut Street, and he had a hunch. Again, his instincts were right; one block over from Walnut was a street called Timberline. If it was the street that Creighton mentioned in his notes, it placed Penton in the neighborhood where Roxann met the bogeyman.

CHAPTER EIGHTEEN

August 6, 2002

The sticky hot days of deep summer had seized the Gulf Coast and immediately assaulted the three detectives like a warm sponge to the face when they stepped out of the car in front of the ramshackle house. The entire dirt-poor neighborhood on the outskirts of the tiny Mississippi town of Bay of St. Louis could have used a coat of paint and a yard-cleaning, but they weren't there on vacation or to look at the scenery.

Stiff after riding all day and covering nearly six hundred miles in a mid-size sedan with two other large men, Sweet stretched his long frame and glanced at the unpainted house. The yard was overrun with weeds, the front screen door was partly off its hinges, and the screen was torn. There was no sign of life, and he wondered if anybody was home.

Three months had passed since the trip to Ohio that had nearly been a bust when Sunnycalb decided to play games and make his demands. It had turned out to be a blessing in disguise because the result was they'd cast the net farther and come up with inmates Tony Baker and Tim Creighton, neither of them pedophiles, who both would make good witnesses.

Since that trip, two of the three recalcitrant informants had undergone changes of heart; apparently time in the hole could be persuasive. Korecky had been the first to call and apologize; he said he'd cooperate with no more demands. He also offered that "there is another inmate who has information about the cases. He does not really want to talk to you right now, but I'm working on him, and I think he may come around."

The former television evangelist Wasmus told prison authorities he didn't want to talk to the Texas detectives anymore. But a week after Korecky changed his mind, Sunnycalb called to say he, too, was sorry and would cooperate without asking for anything.

Sweet had no choice but to accept Sunnycalb's apology and then act like everything was cool between them. Even with the testimony of the other informants, he was the reason they'd gotten as far as they had, and he had the most information—sometimes being the sole link that tied one inmate's details to another. His testimony would be vital at a trial.

"Playing nice" with Sunnycalb rankled Sweet. But the incident was a good reminder that the twice-convicted pedophile couldn't be trusted, even if he could be believed. Sunnycalb was taking a chance exposing a brutal sexual predator who murdered children, but he was doing it for his own ends.

Now, as Sweet walked up to the house in Bay of St. Louis, his mind was on another witness. Someone who wasn't a convict and couldn't be accused by a defense attorney of trying to make a deal in exchange for testifying against Penton. Someone who had actually been in the clutches of the killer and lived to talk about it. He'd finally gotten the okay from his captain to travel to Mississippi to interview Tiffany Ibarra.

As soon as he received permission, Sweet called Bradshaw to see if he could accompany him. The

Mesquite detective had eagerly agreed and brought Phillips with him. Although Ibarra's story was more important to the Proctor case—both girls were abducted from the same area in Dallas several days apart—the detectives knew that all of their cases were stronger when they were working all three of them together. The Proctor case didn't directly help the Meeks or Reyes cases, but as part of the whole, it strengthened them all.

When they left the Dallas area, the detectives didn't head directly for Bay of St. Louis. First, they drove two hundred and seventy miles to Fort Smith, Arkansas, to talk to one of Penton's former girlfriends he'd mentioned to Sunnycalb and Creighton. It was a loose end they had to tie up, but she really didn't have much to say.

The next day they turned the car around and headed south another five hundred and eighty miles to Bay of St. Louis, a town of about nine thousand inhabitants on the Gulf Coast. Nine hours after they started, they walked up to the Ibarra home, where they were met at the battered screen door by Tiffany's mom, Theresa. Sweet explained why they had come, but she shook her head. "Honey, y'all just missed her. She moved with her boyfriend to Batesville, Arkansas."

The news was deflating. For the second time that summer, Sweet wondered how he was going to explain spending all that money on a road trip with nothing to show for it. He called his supervisor, Lt. Keith Thompson, who to his credit told Sweet to "do what you need to do." Bradshaw's supervisors told him the same thing.

It was too late to start for Batesville, so the detectives decided they'd spend the night in Bay of St. Louis. The extra time gave them a chance to talk to Theresa Ibarra.

Over the course of several hours, she told them

about that day her daughter called her and said that a man had kidnapped her on the way to school. She also talked about its sad aftermath. Tiffany had survived, but she'd never been the same, said her mother. She blamed her daughter's later problems with drug abuse and mental issues on the trauma of that day and then the days that followed when her classmate, Christie Proctor, disappeared. "She used to wake up from nightmares. She said she saw him in her dreams."

Tiffany wasn't the only one in her family haunted by the memory. Her mother could recall almost word for word the statements she and her daughter had given to the police. Aware of the old maxim that it's easy to remember the truth but difficult to recall a lie, especially after so much time had passed, Sweet knew she was being honest. But he didn't rely just on his gut instinct as a detective.

As with so many other aspects of this case, he had worked at linking the pieces so that together they formed an unbreakable chain leading to the conviction of Penton. Part of that was getting rid of the weak links. While the detectives were talking to Tiffany's mother, her father, Carlos, came home from work. According to what Penton told Sunnycalb, Carlos Ibarra paid him to kidnap his daughter in order to scare her from being friendly to strangers. The detectives didn't believe it but had to ask Carlos if it was true. As expected, he angrily denied the allegation. "Hell no, I'd never do that to my daughter," he cursed.

The detectives left for Batesville the next day. It was getting to be a long trip, cramped in the sedan, eating on the run, and no one had thought to pack enough extra clothing for an extended journey. But finally, they pulled up to another home, this time in a pleasant, middle-class neighborhood, where a young woman was waiting for them in the driveway.

Surprisingly, Sweet recognized Tiffany Ibarra. She looked a lot like her childhood photograph, just older.

At first, she didn't invite them into the house. Her mother had called her and said they'd be on their way, but she and her boyfriend had moved in with his family, and she apparently didn't want to talk in front of them. So they spoke for a few minutes outside, mostly about the detectives' visit with her mother and father.

Then, her boyfriend's mother poked her head out of the house and invited them all to come in. Tiffany sat down across a coffee table from the detectives and recounted her story. It was obvious that even fourteen years later, she was still frightened. She'd also been dealing all that time with survivor's guilt; Christie Proctor had been a classmate, and even as a child, Tiffany was aware that she had escaped a similar horrific fate.

Tiffany didn't talk about her drug abuse; most people won't when talking to a police officer, even detectives who were not interested in their lifestyle choices. But she did say that she'd been haunted her entire life by Penton, and it was clear to them that she'd suffered long-term mental health issues because of what happened when she was ten years old.

Recalling her meeting with detectives Grisham from Plano and Martha Sanders from Dallas, Tiffany repeated her earlier observation that she believed that the Proctor case had been resolved when Penton was convicted in Ohio. She didn't know that nothing had been done in Texas about the man she'd identified as her abductor.

Sweet placed a binder on the coffee table. In it was a page with another lineup containing six photographs of men, including a different picture of Penton than the one Grisham had used. He had barely opened the notebook to the lineup page, and it was still upside down from Tiffany's vantage point, but she immediately leaned forward and tapped the photograph of Penton.

"That's him," she said without hesitation.

"Wait a minute; let me turn it around so you can see it better," Sweet said.

"You don't need to," Tiffany responded. "That's him. I will never forget his face. I still see him as clearly in my dreams as I did on the day he grabbed me."

It took all of Sweet's self-control to not give away his feelings regarding Tiffany's identification of Penton. A positive identification like she'd just made was a detective's dream. Tiffany Ibarra may have messed up her life with drugs, but she had never forgotten the face of the man who'd warned her, *"If I ever see you alone again, I won't let you go!"* Whatever demons she struggled with, Tiffany had pointed a damning finger at a killer and done it without hesitation and with a good deal of courage.

Sweet was excited by what it all meant. Almost all the other evidence against Penton was based on the word of convicts—a collection of pedophiles, rapists, and murderers no jury would like, especially after a defense attorney tore into their criminal records and character. But Tiffany Ibarra was an eyewitness, herself a victim, and a sympathetic witness the jurors would believe. He could imagine her someday taking the witness stand in a courtroom and identifying Penton with the same certainty as she'd pointed him out in his notebook, giving a name and a face to the bogeyman who had haunted her dreams.

As the detectives got back in the car for the six-hour drive back to Dallas, Sweet imagined the day when he'd also take the stand and describe for a jury the circumstances surrounding Tiffany Ibarra's identification of the man who ran her down on Waterfall Lane intending to rape and murder her. *"She picked him out before I could turn the notebook around. She pointed to him and said, 'That's him. I will never forget ...'"*

CHAPTER NINETEEN

October 21, 2002

Two months after Tiffany Ibarra pointed to a photograph of her childhood bogeyman, Sweet, Bradshaw, Phillips, and Meeks, as well as Sweet's supervisor, Lt. Thompson, flew back to Ohio to follow up on Dallas County Assistant District Attorney Greg Davis' request that they re-interview all the inmate informants.

Although they had not formally presented their cases to the Dallas County District Attorney's Office for prosecution, they had all worked with Davis in the past and respected him. Davis was the chief prosecutor for the Dallas DAO and likely would be trying the case. He tended to get the high-profile death penalty cases and won most of them. They agreed it would be a good time to run what they had past him. After watching a PowerPoint presentation of the three cases put together by Don Phillips and Billy Meeks, Davis said he wanted them to interview all of the informants again and get written statements.

Arriving in Ohio, the detectives split up into teams and headed out on their assigned tasks. Sweet, Meeks, and Thompson drove to Akron, where they met with a former inmate named Marlon Mitchell. He admitted that he'd been in a cell with Penton but didn't remember him talking about any murders. Sweet got the impression that he just didn't want to get involved.

Sweet and Thompson then continued on to Lima to interview James Doan, who was in prison there. Doan was more cooperative and repeated the story they'd heard time after time. Penton liked talking about raping and killing kids and seemed to "get off" on it. He didn't have a lot of specific information or recall any names of victims. However, he did say that Penton spent a lot of time talking to another inmate, a former cop named Howard Guiher, a name Sweet had heard before from Korecky as someone who might have some information.

Meanwhile, Bradshaw and Phillips drove to north Columbus to talk to Albert Mulligan, who'd been in the jail when Penton was arrested for murdering Nydra Ross. They'd been able to reach Mulligan beforehand by phone, and he agreed to meet them on a street corner.

Columbus PD Det. Sheasby had sent Bradshaw a drawing that Mulligan made while in a cell with Penton. Mulligan's daughter had died young, and the drawing was of a young girl ascending to heaven. However, as Mulligan now explained, Penton had taken the drawing and put breasts on the child, then added a merry-go-round and swingset. The killer had finished by sketching a lake on the page.

"I asked him about the lake," Mulligan told the detectives, as he handed them the drawing. "He said it was in Texas."

Like so many of the others who'd been exposed to Penton's brutal sexual fantasies, Mulligan said the killer's eyes would almost glass over as he recalled the murders in vivid detail. The monster truly loved reliving the pain, horror, and suffering he'd inflicted on children. He also told Mulligan that there were "four or five bodies in Texas" that could be linked to him.

After interviewing the former inmates, the teams met up and drove back to the house in Columbus where Penton and his family once lived. Davis wanted them to tear up every board in the attic and see if there was something they'd missed the first time. This time, they found costume jewelry, the sort little girls would wear, beneath the floorboards.

Bradshaw had forgotten about the necklace that Christi Meeks sometimes wore. The family wasn't sure if she had it on that day, but now he wondered if Penton had kept a memento and stashed it with others beneath the floorboards.

Sweet also wondered if the trinkets belonged to one of Penton's known victims or some child they'd not yet identified. He was absolutely convinced that Penton was a serial killer, even if he did not quite match all of the criteria noted by the FBI profiler for Ohio authorities in the Nydra Ross case. But they knew more now than the profiler had back then.

Some of the FBI assessment of Penton was spot on. Sweet and his colleagues knew from the prison informants that Penton was *"a sexual sadist who set up his fantasies in his mind before finding a victim to carry it out."* And one who would *"dispose of a body in a preplanned place."*

They had no evidence that he'd ever used a vacant house. But he had assaulted and murdered the girls in remote places he'd scouted out and felt were immune from discovery. He'd also disposed of their bodies in such a way as it had taken three months to find the remains of Christi Meeks, two years to locate Christie Proctor, and one year to find Roxanne Reyes.

They'd found no evidence that he recorded or videotaped his crimes, but he certainly enjoyed reliving and describing them to the extent that he might as well have had a film projector in his head.

There was no proof that Penton had been sexually abused as a child, but Sweet recalled the interview with Penton's sister, Amanda, and her remarks about the man in the Big Brother organization, a man who had never married but had shown a special interest—including overnight excursions—in Penton from childhood until he quit high school and joined the Army.

As predicted by the FBI profile, he'd lived with his mother following the murder of his son in Texas. The killer's sister, Amanda, also had claimed that Penton hit and otherwise cruelly abused his first wife, Katherine, including when she was pregnant with the son he eventually shook to death for crying. Bradshaw had located Katherine and spoke to her on the telephone. She told him about Penton killing their child and confirmed her former sister-in-law's recollection of how he'd abused her.

Because the bodies of the three victims in Texas were too badly decomposed when found, there was no physical evidence of whether Penton engaged in anal intercourse or bondage, which the FBI profiler said he would do "*because his sexual thrill is fear of the victim.*"

The informants told them that Penton claimed that he sometimes kept his victims alive for several days, sexually assaulting them at will. There were also the photographs of children found in his cell on which he'd written the letter "A" for anal assault.

Julia Diaz, Michael Meeks, and Tiffany Easter had reported that Penton would attempt to lure a child, such as with a promise of cookies or candy. But contradicting the FBI report, the detectives also knew from Diaz and Tiffany Ibarra that he would also chase and physically restrain his intended victims, even if other people were nearby.

Penton had killed Nydra Ross by strangling her as the profiler indicated. The bodies of the Texas victims were too decomposed to establish a cause of death, but it was not by stabbing or gunshot.

As the FBI profile had suggested, after Nydra Ross went missing, Penton had volunteered to help search for her. However, in most of the cases they knew about besides Ross, Penton had grabbed his victim and disappeared; perhaps he'd only changed in the Ross case because he knew her uncle and was trying to divert suspicion from himself.

Unlike the FBI profiler, Sweet was convinced that Penton fit the mold of a serial killer. Sweet knew that Penton's methods varied only by the smallest of details: he'd lure or snatch his victim; drive her somewhere he felt safe to sexually assault her for days; then strangle her and leave the body in a remote area.

The profiler didn't believe that Penton was a serial killer because he didn't *"strike regularly ... as in once a month."* However, the profiler wasn't aware of the other murders, or Sunnycalb's claim that Penton boasted of having killed fifty or more children. Even if the real number was half that, as Sweet suspected, or even a third, it meant he had killed regularly and often. Now, they had to do everything in their power to make sure he never killed again, and that the families of those he had murdered got the answers they deserved.

Leaving Penton's former home in Columbus, the detectives drove to the Warren Correctional Facility. There, they again broke into teams; this time Sweet and Meeks began by interviewing Korecky, while Bradshaw and Phillips talked to a potential new witness and former cellmate of Penton whose murderous ways overshadowed even their suspect's. His name was Donald Harvey, also known across the country to the media and public as "The Angel of Death."

Korecky repeated his assertions that Penton had talked about attacking little girls in Texas, Louisiana, and Arkansas. But now he added that his former cellmate also claimed to have victims in Indiana, which reminded Sweet of another case that had been in the news a few months earlier.

During his conversations with Sunnycalb, the informant had often brought up the names of other alleged victims. Limited in time and resources, Sweet had to concentrate on the Texas cases, but he occasionally put in a telephone call to other law enforcement agencies to fill them in on cases that fell in their jurisdictions. One of those was the abduction of six-year-old Shannon Sherrill who had disappeared in October 1986 from her mother's yard in Thorntown, Indiana.

In July, the Sherrill case suddenly exploded back into the national spotlight when an apparently "mentally ill" woman named Donna Walker came forward claiming to be the long lost child. She'd pulled off the hoax for several days before being exposed, causing Shannon's family to get their hopes up, only to have them dashed.

Sweet wasn't surprised that Walker's claims proved to be false. Since early in their conversations, Sunnycalb had been saying Penton abducted and murdered the girl, and the detective believed him. He'd even tried calling the Thorntown Marshal's Office several times to pass on Sunnycalb's information. After identifying himself and the purpose of his call, he'd been told that someone would get back to him, but no one ever did. Apparently a seventeen-year-old case wasn't a high priority.

Most of the rest of what Korecky said just repeated what he'd told them the first time. However, he did add that Penton said he initially wanted to abduct the older child, Julia Diaz, but she ran away, so he'd settled for Roxann. That bit of information was important to Sweet because it matched Julia's description of what happened that day. Again, more links formed in the chain.

Korecky's assertion that Penton was really after Julia Diaz also taught Sweet a lesson about not letting his personal feelings get in the way of his investigation. Ever since he started talking to Sunnycalb, the informant had said the same thing: Penton wanted Diaz. But it wasn't until Sunnycalb wrote down his official statement that he also added that Penton had actually searched the apartment complex looking for Julia.

When he read the statement from Sunnycalb, Sweet recalled the police report taken from Wanda Huggins. She was the witness who told the police that she'd seen a strange man walking through the apartment complex on the afternoon of the abduction and that he'd run away after she made eye contact. But no one had ever followed up on the information.

So in September, Sweet had gone looking for her. The first thing he learned was that she was a drunk and no one took her seriously. He still wanted to talk to her and finally found her living in a mobile home park in Terrell, Texas.

Sweet called her and asked her if she recalled the day Roxann Reyes was abducted. She was an older woman, but she repeated the same story she'd told a police officer fourteen years earlier.

"Did a detective ever follow-up and talk to you about this?" he asked.

"No."

Sweet was shocked. It didn't make sense that no one had questioned an eyewitness or showed her a photo lineup to try to identify the man she saw. *"Do you think you'd remember his face if you saw a photograph of him?"*

"I might."

Sweet told her he wanted to come see her right away, and she gave him directions. Forty-five minutes later, he walked up to the door of her mobile home and knocked. An old, gray-haired woman answered.

"Hello," he said. *"I'm Detective Sweet with the Garland Police Department."*

Huggins looked confused. *"I haven't done anything in Garland,"* she protested.

Sweet realized that the old woman didn't remember talking to him forty-five minutes earlier and thought she was in trouble for something in Garland. *How in the world is she going to remember Penton's face from fourteen years ago*, he wondered. He was not very optimistic when he explained why he was there.

She suddenly seemed to remember talking to him and invited him in. He showed her the lineup, and to his surprise, she instantly pointed to the photograph of Penton. *"I'm sure that's him,"* she said.

It was a positive identification, but Sweet wasn't excited about it. She couldn't even remember a conversation she'd had less than an hour before. He left thinking that he probably should get a sworn statement from her but decided that it was probably blind luck that she'd picked Penton's photograph.

However, now, a month after he'd dismissed Wanda Huggins as an unreliable witness, a third person, Korecky, had corroborated what Julia Diaz had told police about Roxann's kidnapper chasing her through the apartment complex. Whatever issues Huggins had with alcohol, she'd positively identified the man she saw in the apartment complex as David Penton. But no one had believed her, not even Sweet. It was a valuable lesson not to judge witnesses because of their lifestyles. He resolved to visit Huggins again and get a sworn statement from her.

After talking to Korecky, Sweet and Meeks met up again with Bradshaw and Phillips, who'd been interviewing Donald Harvey. The notorious Angel of Death was believed to have murdered between thirty-six and fifty-seven adults from 1970 to 1987. Most of his victims were patients in hospitals where he worked as an orderly, but he also murdered his homosexual lovers, friends, and neighbors who got on his bad side. His favorite means of execution was poison, though he'd also resorted to suffocation and once even impaled a patient by shoving a coat hanger up the man's catheter. When the police finally caught up to him, and he knew they'd read his carefully detailed diary, he confessed in order to escape facing the death penalty; instead he was sentenced to four consecutive twenty-year sentences.

According to Bradshaw and Phillips, Harvey didn't have much to say about Penton except that he didn't like him because he believed Penton was a pedophile. "I asked him why he thought Penton was a pedophile," Bradshaw recalled, "and he said it was because Penton had a small penis and 'all those types of people do.'"

Harvey didn't cell long with Penton and had asked to be moved. "I don't think he would have put up with Penton or paid him much mind," Bradshaw said.

Next up for Sweet and Meeks was Howard Guiher, the inmate Korecky had told him might have some information and that he was *"working on"* getting him to come forward. Guiher had called Sweet in September and said that at first he didn't want to get involved. Like Creighton, he was a former police officer and was twenty-five years old when he was convicted of having sex with a sixteen-year-old girl. It didn't matter that she'd told him she was of the age of consent; the prosecutor and judge had thrown the book at him. As a result, he was bitter about the justice system.

"But my conscience has been bothering me," he'd said during the call to Sweet. *"So if I can help, I will."*

Guiher didn't want to talk on the telephone, but he was waiting for them when they arrived at the prison and ready to tell them what he knew. He said he'd been listening to Penton's horror stories since 1994, when they were put in the same cell together. They were both into martial arts and sometimes sparred, but Guiher didn't like Penton personally.

He said his former cellmate used a lot of drugs in prison, especially marijuana and the cold medicine Sudafed, which contains the drug pseudoephedrine that can be used to manufacture meth. However, better than any drug to Penton was talking about raping and killing little girls.

Guiher said Penton told him that he stalked the neighborhoods around elementary schools and apartment complexes in low-income areas. Penton said he liked black, Asian, and Hispanic children best, and described them as "throwaway kids" because nobody other than their families would care what happened to them or put much effort into tracking down their killer. "He said he used to punch the girls in the stomach to knock the wind out of them and keep them from screaming when he grabbed them."

Inwardly, Sweet cringed at the statement and

wondered what sort of animal could hit an unsuspecting child so hard as to leave her gasping and defenseless in order to abduct, rape, and murder her. The detective always tried not to react to what a witness or suspect told him so that they wouldn't zero in and say what they thought he wanted to hear. But sometimes it was all he could do not to let his feelings show when he heard descriptions of Penton's brutality.

Guiher said that initially he didn't believe Penton's stories because he seemed to alter the details sometimes and couldn't keep his stories straight. For instance, one day he'd talked about raping and murdering a girl named "Christy" and leaving her body beneath a mattress he'd set on fire. But the next day he said that he'd thrown "Christy's" body in a lake.

"I told him he was full of shit," Guiher said, "because he was changing his stories. But he said he was talking about two different girls named Christy."

Sweet exchanged looks with the other detectives. They didn't say anything to Guiher, but Christie Proctor's body was left under a burning mattress, and Christi Meeks had been thrown from a cliff into Lake Texoma.

According to Guiher, one of Penton's stories described how he'd been pulled over by a Mesquite police officer in a patrol car while he had Christi Meeks still alive in the trunk of his car. "He said he was going to kill the officer if he asked to look in the trunk," Guiher recalled. "But the officer let him go."

What Guiher revealed next was even more chilling. He said that Penton dreamed of getting out of prison to rape and kill more little girls. He'd even spent some time considering how to change his methods for subduing the children. Instead of punching them in the stomach, he explained, he'd use an electric stun gun to render them helpless.

After speaking to Guiher, who'd come across as the most reliable of all the informants, the Texas lawmen felt better than ever about their case. Now they had two former cops—granted one of them a murderer and the other in prison for sexual assault on a minor—who corroborated the stories of the other inmates, yet with enough differences and added detail to make them credible.

What's more, Guiher didn't know Sunnycalb. Add the inmates' accounts to Tiffany Ibarra's identification of Penton as her abductor and Julia Diaz's description of Roxann's killer with the large mole above his right eyebrow, and the case was getting better by the day.

Next up was Tim Creighton, who repeated what he'd originally told them about Penton's boasts. He warned them that Penton was "very aware" that he was being investigated for the Texas murders.

Actually, the detective already knew that Penton was conscious of the fact that they were after him; prison authorities had been intercepting Penton's mail and making copies for them. The inmates were like an old ladies' quilting group, gossiping and talking about the detectives, and word got back to their suspect. Not only did he know they were investigating him, he knew his enemies by name.

Now, Creighton said, Penton was frightened. "It's funny," he said. "For years he's been bragging to anybody who'll listen about raping and murdering those little girls. But now, he says it was all a lie and that he'd never hurt a child."

CHAPTER TWENTY

May 12, 2003

In the spring of 2003, Christi Meeks, Christie Proctor, and Roxann Reyes should have been young women filled with the hopes and dreams of youth. They might have been in college or graduating to begin careers, ready to make a difference in the world. Or they could have been married and happily looking forward to having children of their own. Or maybe just enjoying life, finding their way, while their families watched them grow up, blossom into adults, attending their graduations and weddings, and holding grandbabies.

Instead, a monster who thought of them as throwaways had ripped the girls out of their innocent childhoods, subjected them to unfathomable terror and pain, and then choked the life out of them as they struggled. Deprived of the love and comfort of their families, they'd died at the hands of a loathsome stranger, and their bodies dumped like garbage far from those who prayed for miracles and homecomings.

Yet, they weren't forgotten. Not by their families. Not by Texas lawmen Gary Sweet, Bruce Bradshaw, Don Phillips, Billy Meeks, and the supervisors who supported their efforts. At times, the pace of the investigation was frustrating, but even with all the holdups, they stayed focused on the end goals: making sure Penton never got out of prison and giving the families of the murdered girls the answers to the questions that had plagued them for all those years.

In some ways, a lucky break helped the cause of justice. Penton made a rare mistake when he murdered Nydra Ross. Previously, he'd been so careful—whether it was scouting out where he'd hunt and where he'd murder his victims and dump their bodies, making sure to cross jurisdictional lines, and selecting children to whom he had no connection. But he'd worked with Nydra's uncle and was drinking and smoking crack cocaine at the man's house the night before he kidnapped, raped, and killed Nydra.

Even though he'd pretended to help search for her, he'd immediately become the primary suspect, especially after blood was discovered in his van. Then, after Nydra's remains were found and he was arrested, he'd boasted about his crimes to other inmates. The mistakes cost him; otherwise, the bogeyman might have still been on the loose, hunting for his next victims.

However, catching Penton because of his mistake didn't mean that he was done killing little girls. The prosecutors in Ohio could have lost the case, or agreed to a plea agreement that would have resulted in a lesser sentence for Penton. Even though he'd received a life sentence, he was up for parole at 70 years of age and still capable of evil. Or he might get out even earlier, depending on the vagaries of the justice system. If nothing else, Sweet wanted to tack convictions in Texas onto the Ohio prison sentence; but he really he wanted Penton to at least face the possibility of a death sentence.

In several past murder cases investigated by Sweet, the killers had been sentenced to life without parole and he'd been good with that. But some murderers were so evil, their crimes so beyond the pale of human redemption, that he believed a death sentence was the only appropriate sentence. Michael Giles would have been one of those, but his age had saved him from even consideration for a death sentence. Brutal monsters like Giles and Penton could not be rehabilitated. Penton's taste for raping and murdering children wasn't something that could be cured.

However, Sweet had another reason for hoping Texas prosecutors would seek the death penalty. In Texas, a death sentence wasn't an empty threat. The average stay on death row for the United States as a whole was 17 years, and in states like California twenty or more years; but in Texas, the average was ten years, and some killers in the 21st century had been executed by lethal injection in less than a year. Part of that was due to a "streamlined" system that cut down on appeals; other reasons included a largely pro-death penalty population in which "frontier justice" was still an acceptable part of the culture, as well as that of elected appellate judges and parole boards, who reflected the will of their constituents.

Sentenced to death in Texas, Penton would not have the opportunity to grow old, and the killer would know that. Sweet thought that by holding the possibility of a death sentence over Penton's neck, the coward might be willing to trade his life in exchange for telling authorities about his other victims, including helping them locate the remains. He'd still never get out of prison, and the families of missing and murdered children would have their answers.

If that was the price of Penton avoiding being strapped to a cold, steel table and put down like a rabid dog, Sweet could live with it. But it would all have to start by putting a case together so that the District

Attorney's Office could indict Penton for the murder of three little girls in Texas.

So, Sweet and the other detectives dutifully spent the months between October 2002 and the spring of 2003 running down leads, interviewing and re-interviewing witnesses, conferring with each other, updating Assistant District Attorney Davis, and, of course, talking to Sunnycalb on the telephone.

Sunnycalb even talked about getting out of prison and moving to Garland, where he could help Sweet work on the cases. "Maybe you could help me find a place to live?"

The last thing he wanted to do was help a two-time sex offender move to his town, but Sweet didn't discourage him. In fact, when Sunnycalb asked about Texas sex offender registration laws, he had one of his department's sex offender investigators talk to him.

Finally in May, seven years after he'd walked into the "murder closet" as a new detective and three years since he'd first spoken to Sunnycalb, Sweet was ready to talk to Penton. In preparation for the meeting, he read everything he could find about psychopaths. He knew that by definition they lacked a conscience, so appealing to his sense of morality wouldn't work.

Psychopaths know right from wrong—so they don't fit the legal definition of criminally insane and, therefore, not responsible for their actions—they just don't care. They see themselves as entitled to act as they do. They tend to be consummate liars and hide their true natures behind a façade that protects them from discovery; that's why when a serial killer such as Ted Bundy or John Wayne Gacy is arrested, invariably a neighbor, family member, or girlfriend will tell the media that they are surprised because *"he was such a nice guy."*

Most serial killers have big egos and believe that they're smarter than their pursuers, which went into Sweet's plan for talking to Penton. He knew that Penton liked to brag about his crimes, and while he didn't expect Penton would confess outright, there was a chance that his inflated image of himself would cause him to slip up.

Sweet and Bradshaw learned every detail about Penton's life and character that they could. They'd agreed that they weren't going to let him deny killing the girls; every time he tried, they'd throw it back in his face that they knew he was guilty.

As far as Bradshaw was concerned, he truly thought that he was going to meet the devil, himself. He'd shown his wife, Gail, a photograph of Penton, and she'd remarked that he had the same crazy look in his eyes as infamous killer Charles Manson. The darkness that had entered their lives on January 19, 1985, had a name, David Elliot Penton. But Bradshaw was also sure that God was with Sweet and him and that they would prevail.

This time, the team of detectives flew into Columbus and drove to Marion, Ohio, where Penton had been transferred. He knew the other inmates were talking about him now, and he had been moved for their protection.

The prison didn't have an interview room, so Sweet and Bradshaw were waiting for him when Penton entered the cell near the front of the facility normally used for consultations between defense attorneys and their clients. He frowned and looked confused; he didn't know who they were or why he'd been brought to the room.

"Have a seat," Sweet said, indicating a chair across the small table from where they sat.

Only then did the detectives introduce themselves, and Penton's confused look turn to one of fear. He knew their names, and the blood drained from his face; then, a dark wet spot grew at his crotch, and a stench filled the room. Bradshaw would never forget the smell; strong and pungent, it reminded him of the odor of cat or goat urine. Later, he and Sweet would give it another name, "the smell of fear." Their appearance had literally scared the piss out of him.

Penton crossed his legs and turned away to hide his humiliation. The detectives pretended not to have noticed. They wanted to talk to him, and with an ego like his, he might have shut down from embarrassment.

"I'm glad you guys are here," Penton blurted out before the detectives could say another word. His already pasty face now ashen, he continued, "I wanted to tell you that I didn't do these crimes I've been accused of."

Sweet stopped him by holding up his hand. "You misunderstand," he said, his tone matter-of-fact. "We didn't come here to talk about whether or not you did it; we know you did it. We just wanted to meet you before we bring you back to Texas and kill you."

Penton visibly quailed at Sweet's threat. Terror swam in his pale blue eyes. "I didn't do anything," he protested.

Sweet shrugged and repeated himself. "We aren't here to talk about it. Like I said, we just wanted to meet you before we bring you back to Texas to kill you."

Bradshaw leaned forward. "David, we know you did it."

Penton went silent. He squirmed in his seat, his movements agitated. They'd been warned by prison officials that Penton was into martial arts, and Sweet wondered if he was about to explode. Part of him wished he would so that he could beat the crap out of the child killer, but he knew his ultimate goal would be better served by getting Penton to talk. They also didn't want to get into an *"I didn't do it. Yes, you did"* argument. So Sweet used the moment to change the tone of the confrontation by appealing to his quarry's ego with a compliment.

"David, I give you credit," he said shaking his head. "You were very good at it. Look how long it took us to catch you."

Penton smiled and seemed pleased by the compliment, though he still professed his innocence. The detectives pressed on, talking a lot about the murders and what they thought he'd done. During some parts of the conversations, he was animated, moving his head and hands around as if he couldn't keep them still. But when they talked about the crimes, he'd sit absolutely still and not say a word. Sweet got the sickening impression that he was reliving his acts as they discussed them

At one point, Bradshaw said, "What if I told you we searched your house in Columbus and found something in the attic?"

"I would say that was a lie," Penton responded. "I never took any souvenirs. I'm smarter than that. And if I had taken anything, all I'd have to do is call my mom; she loves me and would get rid of anything for me."

It took every bit of willpower the detectives had not to react to Penton's statement. He'd just confessed, apparently without knowing it, but they let him keep talking, hoping he would make other incriminating statements. He soon rewarded their patience.

"You can't have anything but circumstantial evidence," Penton said then smirked. "I'm not stupid; I didn't leave any evidence."

Again, the detectives were stunned by the admission. Sweet had always made it a practice to really listen to what people said; sometimes they'd tell the truth without knowing it, and Penton had just done it twice. But again, he didn't react and just asked another question. "Did you use a condom?"

Now, Penton realized what he'd said and its implications. He stuttered and tried to backtrack. "I meant that I didn't leave any evidence because I didn't do it."

The two detectives talked to Penton for a couple of hours, a lot of it playing mind games. They told him that the prosecutor they were working with in Texas, Greg Davis, had sent so many murderers to Death Row that he was known as "The Grim Reaper."

"If he wants you dead, you're going to die," Sweet said.

They repeated the nickname so often that Penton himself started using it, at one point even humorously. "Tell The Grim Reaper that I will confess if he pays off my debt to the state of Ohio and gets me a color TV for my cell."

"We're not here to play 'Let's Make a Deal,'" Sweet replied, which got a laugh even from Penton.

The cops and the killer danced around getting him to confess to the killings outright. But he shook his head. "I ain't going to say shit while my mom's alive," he told them.

It was getting late in the day, so they decided to end the conversation by telling Penton that they'd see him soon in Texas. When the inmate left the room, the detectives let down their guard. They believed that the bogeyman had as much as confessed, but would it hold up in court?

"We need to record him," Sweet said. Recording interviews was optional in Texas at that time and not commonly used, so he had not thought of it going into this interview and not knowing that Penton was going to be so talkative or slip up under questioning. They decided that they'd try to borrow one from prison authorities and interview Penton again the next day.

All four detectives returned to the prison in the morning. This time, Phillips and Meeks joined the other two in the interview room. When Sweet and Bradshaw were talking to Penton, they'd gone through the killer's cell, noting how neat and tidy he kept his living space. But they'd also discovered one chilling item—a plastic bag containing clean "civilian clothes, neatly bundled with a piece of string and hidden in Penton's cell. It had all the markings of an "escape bag," but whether he had a plan or it was "just in case," they detectives could only guess. Now having seen how excited their colleagues were, Phillips and Meeks wanted a chance to question Penton, too.

When the killer was brought in and introduced to the two new detectives, there was no element of surprise and he controlled his bladder. However, he again proclaimed his innocence. "I would never do anything like that."

Sweet thought there was a difference between saying "I would never do anything like that" and "I didn't do it." He believed that deep down most people, even psychopaths like Penton, have a hard time lying without giving themselves away. By saying *"I wouldn't do that"* instead of *"I didn't do that,"* he was, in his mind, not truly lying. Then, Penton slipped up again. They were talking about his drug use, and Penton told them he was addicted to crack and had in fact been using a lot of it while in Texas during the period of time in question. Suddenly, he said that it was possible he had committed murders, but if so he couldn't remember because he was "too high."

Sweet saw it as a confession. It was another way of saying "I would not do that if I was in my right mind," or "I blacked out and don't remember killing them." That excuse had been used on him a lot over the years, as if the killers thought it made them seem less evil. He'd never believed it before and didn't believe it now.

The interview progressed, with all four detectives shooting questions at the suspect. He didn't have time to think before someone asked him another question. It could have been mass confusion, but there were four good detectives in the room who knew how to play off each other. They even talked about the "bag telephone" that his employer at the time of the Ibarra kidnapping, Wayne Welch, let him use when on the job. Rather than deny knowing anything about the phone, he described it just like Tiffany Ibarra had.

Bradshaw told Penton that he knew what happened to Christi Meeks. Since that day in January 1985, the detective had thought a lot about how the monster's mind worked. He'd worked innumerable cases involving child sexual assault, read everything he could find on what made pedophiles tick, and interviewed dozens of suspects and obtained confessions from many of them. Sometimes it took what he thought of as *"crawling in the ditch with them,"* making them believe that he understood their attraction to young children; that anybody could have the same attraction, or that the child was to blame for *"coming on to them."*

That's where he was headed when he told Penton, "I've been thinking about this for years and years, and what I think happened is you got her in the car, and then when you were having sex with her she started screaming. So you put your hand over her mouth and suffocated, or strangled, her."

Bradshaw intended to crawl in the ditch, pretend he understood Penton's vile thoughts and place the blame on Christi. Try to get him to confess by identifying with him. But as he spoke, he noticed how Penton had grown absolutely still, his eyes glazed over and a slight smile played across his thin lips. *He's reliving it,* the detective thought. *He's getting off on me telling the story.* Horrified, he stopped talking; he wasn't getting in the ditch, he wasn't willing to go there with this particular evil.

The room was absolutely quiet. Bradshaw waited for someone else to go forward in the same vein. But no one spoke; no one else was willing to crawl into that dark chasm with Penton.

This time, when the detectives again told him they would be taking him to Texas to die, Penton just shrugged. "Okay, then I guess I'll die," he said.

Without really knowing why he took the conversation in this direction, unless God was leading him, Sweet asked, "What do you think is going to happen to you after you die?"

Penton's shrugged. "I'm right with God, so I'm not worried."

Although he didn't really believe it, Sweet told Penton that he believed that he was sincere in his beliefs. It was a hard thing to say because the detective could see right through him, but he wanted the killer to know that God could see through his lies, too.

Penton responded by declaring his innocence again. "I'm a man of God."

Sweet sighed and shook his head. Prison authorities had warned the detectives not to get into religious debates with Penton, who, when not boasting about raping and killing children, apparently made a big show of reading the Bible and going to Bible-study classes. *"He'll try to lure you into a discussion to sidetrack you."*

However, Sweet couldn't stand listening to Penton's religious claims any longer. He knew in his heart that Penton was an unrepentant child killer and a liar. Ever since his days as a patrol officer, he'd had plenty of experience dealing with criminals who tried to hide behind religion and jailhouse conversions. And as a deacon in his church and an interim youth minister who read his Bible regularly, he was more than capable of handling his own when it came to *"God talk."* So he stepped out on faith, trusting that God would not let an evil man win this debate.

He began by saying about how much he loved the biblical story of King David and Bathsheba. How David had lusted after Bathsheba, a married woman, to the point where he sent the woman's husband into battle knowing he would die. Meanwhile back in Jerusalem, David, now a murderer, and Bathsheba committed adultery. And that God had punished the couple by causing their newborn son to die. But that David had repented and God had forgiven him, and called him a man after God's own heart, even having committed such serious sins.

As Sweet talked, Penton didn't move. He just sat still, stared, and listened. Even the other detectives were quiet as Sweet spoke confidently and earnestly. "We know you killed these girls, but God will forgive you, and you can be a man after God's own heart," he said.

"But I didn't kill them," protested Penton, breaking his silence.

"David, you're lying, and the Bible says that God

hates a liar," Sweet insisted. "I believe if you have repented these murders, that God will forgive you, just like he forgave King David. But not if you lie to cover up a sin."

Penton looked dazed and at a loss for words. Long after this interview concluded, Sweet would believe that God was speaking through him, or at least helping him find the right words to say. When Penton again weakly insisted that he was innocent, the detective replied, "You can tell us that you're innocent, and you can tell the judge that you're innocent, but someday you will stand before another judge that you won't be able to say that to; He knows everything you've done."

Something clicked in Penton as he shouted, "We will all stand before God. All of us! And you may be standing with me!" He smiled as if he hit a home run at a ballpark.

Sweet nodded, his eyes locked on his opponent's, as he calmly replied, "That's right David, and those little girls will be standing with us, too."

The color that had risen in Penton's face drained away. He froze and just looked at Sweet for a long time, unable to speak. Then, he swallowed hard and bobbed his head. "Good," he said, though his voice was subdued, defeated. "Then they can tell you I didn't do it."

After that, Penton seemed a beaten man, one who knew he couldn't talk his way out of trouble this time. But Sweet wasn't letting him off the ropes. Instead, he repeated the verse from Proverbs he'd responded with since his earliest days as a police officer when criminals tried to pull the God card on him. "*Whoever conceals their sins does not prosper, but the one who confesses and renounces them finds mercy.*"

On that note, it was over. Several intense hours had

passed since they started, but now it was time to end it. Penton looked like a rat trapped in a corner by a terrier; his eyes darted around as if looking for a way to escape, and he couldn't sit still.

"We'll be waiting for you in Texas," Sweet said again as he and the other detectives rose to leave. That's how they left him: alone, knowing he would soon be facing a murder trial with the possibility of a death sentence.

A few minutes later, as the detectives walked out of the prison, Phillips, another born-again Christian police officer, looked at Sweet and grinned. "Dang, I was almost saved back there!"

They all had a good laugh. The train of justice for Roxann Reyes, Christi Meeks, and Christie Proctor was about to pull into the station, and it was time to celebrate.

CHAPTER TWENTY-ONE

June 17, 2003

Three weeks after the bogeyman wet his pants when confronted by a pair of tenacious Texas lawmen, Sweet sat at his desk, waiting for a call, one that in a sense he'd been waiting to hear for seven years. The call to say whether Penton had been indicted in Collin County for the murders of Roxanne Reyes, Christi Meeks, and Christie Proctor.

He was confident the news would be good. He and his colleagues—Bradshaw, Phillips, and Meeks—had done their jobs; they'd put together a case he believed good enough not just to indict Penton, but to convict him. Any doubts he'd had went away after interviewing the killer. And they'd continued tracking down odds and ends up to the day Greg Davis took the evidence before a grand jury to ask them to indict Penton on capital murder charges.

In fact, right after talking to Penton, Sweet and Meeks drove to Minford, Ohio, to speak to Roxann's aunt, Tanya. They were following up on the notes that Tim Creighton had given them about the young woman Penton said he'd visited on Timberline Street in Garland.

Creighton had misheard the street name as "Treeline," but Sweet was convinced Timberline was correct and confirmed it through Roxann's mother, Tammy. He told her about Creighton's note, and she said that she'd lived on Timberline before moving to the apartment complex where her daughter was abducted. She also said that Roxann's father, Sergio, as well as her sister, Tanya, had lived there with her.

Sweet had gone to the neighborhood and walked down the street, knocking on every single door, hoping to find the woman Penton had visited. But most of the people he talked to had not lived there in the mid-1980s, and no one recognized Penton from the photographs.

However, Sweet had a theory on the woman's identity. As soon as Tammy said that her sister, Tanya, had also lived on Timberline, the thought crossed his mind that she was whom Penton and Creighton were referring to; he thought it was worth asking her anyway.

Arriving in Minford, the detectives called ahead and then drove to the neighborhood where Tanya lived. Sitting in the living room of her sparse home, the detectives asked the obviously nervous woman a few easy personal questions, but she wasn't saying much.

Then, Sweet opened his file and showed her the same photo lineup he'd shown to Tiffany Ibarra. Tanya appeared to be looking hard at the photograph of Penton. Sweet and Meeks thought she was on the verge of pointing him out. But after more than a minute of looking at the photograph, she finally shook her head and said she didn't recognize anyone. Disappointed, the detectives got back in their car for the long drive back to Columbus.

After four hours, they decided to stop and spend the night in Waverly. The next morning the detectives were preparing to get on the road to Columbus when they received a call from Marletta Scribner, an investigator with the Collin County DAO who'd traveled with the detectives to Columbus. She said she had just got off the telephone with Tammy Lopez. Apparently, her sister, Tanya, had called her after the detectives had left her house. In tears, Tanya admitted to Tammy that she had recognized one of the men in the photo lineup.

Sweet and Meeks headed back to Minford and Tanya's house. This time, she admitted that she'd recognized one of the men in the photo lineup. She said she used to see him occasionally at one of the drug houses in the neighborhood. "There was a lot of drugs and sex going on in the house," she said, "and I remember him because he was strange. He never had sex with any of the girls, and he used crack cocaine; nobody else in the house was using crack at that time." She said she'd been worried about admitting her drug use to the detectives.

This time, when Sweet showed her the photo lineup, Tanya didn't hesitate. She pointed to the photograph they'd seen her staring at the day before. The photograph of David Penton. "That's him."

After leaving Tanya's, Sweet thought about Penton's comment during the interview that he was using a lot of crack cocaine back in the mid-1980s and that he could have committed the murders but "forgot" because he was so high. He knew that was a bullshit excuse, but his admitted drug use bolstered Tanya's account. She had also corroborated Creighton's story about Penton socializing in the neighborhood where Roxann was abducted.

There were two more items of importance that came about from the trip to Ohio. One of them had to do with a comment Sunnycalb had made to Sweet regarding the abduction of Tiffany Ibarra. He said that Penton had told him he'd been in possession of a "bag phone," the precursor to cell phones, and that he'd let the girl make a call to her mother from it. The phone, according to

Penton, had belonged to his employer, Wayne Welch.

While in Ohio, Sweet and Meeks located Welch's ex-wife, who verified that her former husband had a bag phone and she confirmed that sometimes Penton was given the device to use for work. She said she had kept all the records from the phone company and promised to try to find them.

While a seemingly minor detail, the bag phone was the nexus between what Tiffany and Theresa Ibarra had told police in 1986 and repeated to Sweet, Bradshaw, and Phillips in October, and what Sunnycalb claimed Penton had said. If there had not been a bag phone— if Tiffany had made it all up—then Penton wouldn't have known about it, nor could he have said anything to Sunnycalb in that regard.

The last benefit from that trip to Ohio involved Bradshaw and Phillips. When Sweet and Meeks went to Minford, the other two had returned to the prison in Marion to interview more inmates to see if Penton had boasted of his crimes there. They'd talked to several of Penton's friends, but with no success. The detectives then left to meet up with Sweet and Meeks in Columbus.

However, soon after leaving, the detectives received a call from one of the prison investigators. He said that an inmate named Clay Krcal had just contacted him and asked if the detectives were at the prison to talk about Penton. Apparently, word had got around already. Krcal told the investigator that Penton had talked to him about several murders. The investigator was calling to see if they wanted to return to the prison to speak to the inmate; he didn't have to ask twice.

Krcal was an interesting character. He'd been employed by the National Football League but had embezzled league money, which is how he'd ended up in prison. He was working in the prison library when he got to know Penton, a frequent visitor.

Krcal told Bradshaw and Phillips that Penton had once confessed that he'd killed Nydra Ross and tried to outwit police investigators by taking a hair from a comb belonging to someone else and leaving it on her body. He said Penton told him he'd also tried this trick with murders he'd committed in Texas and North Carolina.

More recently, Penton had come to him asking for help researching modern methods of DNA analysis, Krcal said. A lot had changed in the science between 1988 and 2003, and he was worried that the new technology might get him caught for the Texas murders.

Taken singularly, bits and pieces of evidence and potential testimony, such as Krcal's, didn't amount to much. But as pieces of a larger puzzle, they created a picture of a killer realizing that his boasts about being smarter than the cops might be coming back to haunt him. And Sweet was determined to find as many of those small and large pieces as possible.

In January, he'd followed up on a promise he'd made to himself to correct a past mistake. He drove the forty-five minutes to Wanda Huggins' mobile home and took a sworn statement from the old woman. This time, she did remember him and repeated what she'd told him the first time. Then, finally, it had been time to give the case to Assistant District Attorney Davis to take to the Collin County grand jury.

Originally, the detectives planned to have the case presented to the Dallas District Attorney's Office to seek an indictment. Roxann Reyes and Christie Proctor had both been abducted from that county. However, during the investigation, Davis, who'd been with the Dallas DAO, went to work for the Collin County DAO, and they wanted to keep the cases with him. The remains of Roxann and Christie were found in Collin County so there was no problem with jurisdiction. Because Plano was located in Collin County, Det. Meeks volunteered to do the paperwork necessary to present the cases.

When Collin County District Attorney John Roach announced his office was seeking to charge Penton, he told the *Dallas Morning News* that he was confident the grand jurors would return three murder indictments. *"And if they do that,"* he said for a story that appeared May 22, 2003, *"we intend to seek the death penalty."*

The newspaper talked to the girls' families, who expressed both sadness and gratitude that the day of reckoning was finally at hand. *"Thank you, Lord,"* Linda Meeks, Christi's mother, said. *"It's been a long time coming, a long 18 years. I'm shocked, nervous, scared — all rolled into one."*

She said that she'd suffered an emotional breakdown in the months after her daughter's body was found. She'd buried the horror of the loss so deep *"that I had to have my sister show me where Christi's grave was later on."* But, she said, she never gave up hope. *"I just thought, 'If he doesn't get his day here on earth, he'll get it on judgment day when he leaves this earth.'"*

She added that she hoped that her daughter's death might have helped other potential victims. *"In a roundabout way, it helped bring in media attention and public awareness,"* she said. *"It showed that it could happen to anybody. It's not because you didn't watch your child."*

Christi's father, Mike Meeks, told the newspaper, *"the whole family is hurt and relieved by it all,"* particularly Christi's brother, Michael. *"It's affected my son and he's felt guilty about this for so long. It'll be a great comfort for him."*

Also interviewed by the newspaper, Michael Meeks described the years following his sister's abduction as *"torture. I haven't been able to do anything right in a long time. I need this for myself, and I need this for my children. I think it's going to help a lot."*

Tammy Lopez told the newspaper that prosecuting Roxann's killer after so many years would be a relief. *"I know he's not going to go through the pain like my little girl did — or those other two little girls — but it's comforting to know he'll get what's coming to him."*

Lopez said her family had been waiting for fifteen years for the police to put together the case against Penton. *"My mother and stepfather saw this guy's picture in a paper"* when he was charged with killing Nydra Ross in Ohio. *"It matched a composite drawing released"* by Garland police. *"But I've been told to say no more right now so it won't spoil the case,"* she said. *"I want this guy put down for what he did."*

In a press release, District Attorney Roach praised the police detectives from Garland, Mesquite, and Plano, *"who are to be commended for their dedication, hard work, and coordinated investigation in preparing and presenting these cases for prosecution."*

"The acceptance and prosecution of these cases will serve as notice to anyone who would abduct and murder our children that we will not forget. We will not forget the killer; we will not forget the crime; and we will not forget the victims."

Meanwhile, the detectives who had worked so long and hard on the case waited nervously to hear the outcome of the grand jury proceedings. They were confident of the cases they'd put together. But they knew that there were no guarantees that there would be an indictment, or if there were, that they'd win at trial.

During grand jury proceedings, only the prosecution presents evidence. No defense attorney presents contradicting evidence or cross-examines the witnesses as the defense would at trial. The threshold a prosecutor faces to ask grand jurors to return an indictment also is lower than what would be required to convict a defendant at trial. A conviction in a trial would require that the prosecution prove its case beyond a reasonable doubt after the defense had done its best to dispute the evidence. However, for an indictment, which was necessary to have the defendant charged with the crime and bound over for trial, the prosecution only had to prove that if the prosecution's case was not successfully contradicted by the defense, a trial jury would be likely to find the defendant guilty.

Among those subpoenaed to testify was Penton's mother. If the grand jury indicted Penton, he would be arrested and a defense attorney would be assigned to his case. Davis wanted Penton's mother on the record and under oath before she had a chance to get together with her son's lawyer.

Three weeks after the grand jury began hearing testimony, Sweet's telephone rang. Five years earlier, he'd been the only detective in the office when first one phone and then another rang, until finally Roxann Reyes's mother reached the detective who knew the tragic story hidden in two file boxes of the Garland Police Department murder closet, waiting for someone to care. Others might call it coincidence. He believed it was divine intervention.

This time, the call came straight to him. It was from Greg Davis; the bogeyman was going to be tried for murdering three little girls.

Hanging up with Davis, Sweet punched in another number. It was time to tell Bruce Bradshaw that his long wait was coming to a close.

CHAPTER TWENTY-TWO

January 6, 2004

In August 2003, David Elliot Penton was extradited to Texas to stand trial for the murders of Roxann Reyes, Christi Meeks, and Christie Proctor.

Waiting for him at the Collin County Jail when he arrived were detectives Gary Sweet, Bruce Bradshaw, Don Phillips and Billy Meeks.

They were shocked when they saw Penton in the booking room. He looked as if he'd lost thirty, maybe forty, pounds.

"We told you we were going to bring you back," Bradshaw said when Penton glanced their way. The killer didn't reply, but the distraught look on his face said it all.

Still, the detectives knew the hard part was just beginning. Every detail of their investigation would be analyzed by Penton's defense team. They hoped they had not missed something that would let Penton slip away from justice.

Sweet thought Penton's weight loss was probably due to stress. The defendant had been given an attorney and knew what evidence the detectives had amassed during their investigations. In spite of his claim that he was smarter than those in law enforcement who pursued him, his need to boast about his horrific crimes, the little mistakes he'd made, and then meticulous police work had combined to bring him back to Texas, where he would be facing the death penalty.

His chances of acquittal had not gotten any better since his indictment, either. In fact, the cases against him grew even stronger after news reports about his indictment, including a recent prison mugshot, hit the television broadcasts and the front pages of newspapers throughout Texas. The most significant additions were two more young women who came forward and claimed that Penton had tried to abduct them when they were children, too.

Shortly after Penton was indicted, Bradshaw called Sweet and said a young woman named Tanya Dickerman called him and said that the man shown on the newscast had attempted to kidnap her on November 30, 1987. The date was particularly important because it was the same month and year that Roxann was abducted.

Dickerman told Bradshaw that a man in a gray sedan followed her and her brother to school one morning. Then when school let out, he was waiting. As she walked home alone, he pulled up next to her and asked if she wanted to go with him to buy ice cream.

"She told him 'No,' and ran home," Bradshaw told Sweet. When she got to an alley near her house, the man was still following her, so she ran to a neighbor's home. The neighbor called the police. *"She said when her mom got home from work she found the back door to their house open."*

Seventeen years later, Dickerman saw Penton's photograph on the television news and called Bradshaw. *"That's the guy that tried to get me in the car."*

Bradshaw asked her if a police report was filed in 1987. Dickerman said yes and in fact remembered that he was the detective who had come to her house to interview her about the incident.

"I didn't remember it at first," Bradshaw told Sweet. *"But I went back to the archives and reviewed the report and recalled some of it."* Nobody but Dickerman and her brother saw the stalker, and they didn't get a license plate number; so there was nothing to follow up.

The other caller's name was Amanda Rollins. She told Bradshaw that in early January 1985, she was five years old and playing outside of an apartment complex just six-tenths of a mile from where Christi Meeks was abducted when a man grabbed her. *"She said she kicked him and ran away,"* Bradshaw told Sweet. *"Then she hid in the bushes until he left."*

After Christi disappeared, Bob Holleman interviewed Rollins and her brother, who'd witnessed the attempted abduction. *"There's a copy of the Dallas police report about the incident in the Meeks file, along with Bob's notes,"* Bradshaw said.

He met with Rollins and showed her a photo lineup that included Penton's 1988 mugshot from Ohio, which was different from the photograph shown on the newscast. Without hesitation, she'd pointed to Penton.

All of their lives, the two young women had lived in fear of the bogeyman: that someday he'd come back for them; that he was just waiting. Now they'd been able to put a face and a name to him and, as with Tiffany Ibarra, could point to him from the witness stand and condemn the man who'd haunted their dreams and stood in the shadows of their nightmares.

In addition to interviewing the two young women, Bradshaw had continued following up on his case's loose ends. In November, he'd asked Christi's brother, Michael, to undergo hypnosis to see if that would help him recall anything new. But nothing much had come of it other than the realization that the abduction had haunted the young man all of his life.

Bradshaw and Phillips also tracked down Tiffany Easter, who had been Christi's playmate the day the man lured her friend away. They found her living in Irving, Texas, with children of her own.

Just the sight of Bradshaw, however, caused her to burst into tears. The detective believed that she blamed herself for what happened—after all, she'd been the older child but hadn't been able to save her friend—and seeing him brought back all the haunting memories.

So Bradshaw excused himself and asked Phillips to carry on the interview. Even then, Easter was too distraught to say much. She said that after Christi disappeared, she'd become withdrawn and lived in constant fear that the man who took her friend would come back for her. When Phillips showed her the photo lineup that included Penton, she started crying again but wouldn't point to a photograph.

"You know he's there, don't you?" Phillips asked.

Easter nodded. Eighteen years had passed, but she was still too frightened of the bogeyman to identify him.

Meanwhile, Sweet also made it a point to continue talking to the informants. He spoke almost daily to Sunnycalb, usually about some of the cases in other jurisdictions that Sweet had for the most part set aside to concentrate on the three Texas murders. As a result, he started calling the other law enforcement agencies—such as in Temple, Texas, Thorntown, Indiana, and Pennsylvania—trying to interest them in at least talking to Sunnycalb.

He also stayed in touch with the former cop, Guiher. Of all the inmate informants, he seemed the most credible and likeable; the only one whom Sweet believed was talking about Penton for no other reason than it was the right thing to do.

Sweet spoke a few times about the upcoming trial with Tammy Lopez, who kept thanking him for everything he'd done to find her daughter's killer. He also talked to Julia Diaz to prepare her and try to calm her nerves about facing Penton from the witness stand.

After all the pre-trial hearings and motions, Penton was set to go to trial on January 10. Davis was going to start by trying him for the murder of Roxann Reyes, considered the strongest of the three cases because Sweet had better witnesses and more of them. Some witnesses would be called at each of the trials, such as the inmate informants and Tiffany Ibarra. But Sweet also had Julia Diaz, who could testify about the man in the gray sedan and had described him to police as having the large mole over his right eye, and Wanda Huggins, who'd positively identified Penton as the stranger she saw in the apartment complex that day. There was also Roxann's aunt, Tanya, who could place Penton in a drug house a couple of blocks from the apartment complex.

Sweet's testimony would tie it all together, such as the photographs from Penton's prison notebook and the title to the gray Datsun. From the witness stand, he would testify how all the disparate pieces of evidence and the testimony of all the witnesses when pieced together showed that David Penton was the man who abducted and murdered Roxann Reyes. The other detectives would then add their pieces to the puzzle.

The detectives knew they had strong cases, and Davis seemed confident throughout the many pretrial hearings. Then, just a few days before jury selection was to begin, they received calls asking them to report to the courthouse. They thought it was just another pre-trial hearing or something to do with jury selection.

When they arrived, the detectives were directed to a room where they were surprised to see the families of the victims and the prosecutor. Then Davis broke the news: Penton's defense attorneys claimed to have "new evidence" they said demonstrated that their client was working in Ohio during the time of Roxann's murder.

Sweet didn't say anything, but he knew the "new evidence" was a lie. They had too much on Penton. He was a dead ringer for the composite, down to the mole on his face; Wanda Huggins had seen him in the apartment complex just after the abduction; Tanya saw him there several times before the murder; he'd confessed to numerous inmates and gave accurate details not available through open records. There was too much evidence to doubt the case.

Davis didn't think the "new evidence" was valid, either, but proving it when the trial was just days away could be tough. Going to trial would be risky, he said; all it would take was one juror who believed even a suspect piece of evidence. "And if we lose, we can't retry him again."

Unwilling to take a chance of letting Penton off for the murders in Texas, Davis said, the District Attorney's Office had decided to accept a defense offer. Penton had agreed to plead guilty to the three murder charges and be sentenced to life without parole. Even if Ohio authorities paroled him, they then would turn him over to the Texas Department of Corrections. He'd never get out of prison, but it would eliminate the threat of the death penalty.

Davis said that Penton was on his way to the courthouse to enter his plea. After that, the families could make victim impact statements to the court.

Everyone in the room seemed stunned. The families of the victims weren't asked their opinion before the deal was reached and weren't happy with the decision. Christi's father, Mike Meeks, along with his ex-wife, Christi's mother Linda, got up and walked out of the meeting.

Bradshaw watched Meeks go with regret. He and Holleman had been close to the family, and he could empathize with a man whose five-year-old daughter had been so cruelly taken from him. Now, he felt as if he'd somehow failed Christi's father.

Penton's appearance in court was anti-climatic. He never looked over at the detectives, who had told him they would bring him back to Texas to pay for his crimes. Nor did he reveal any details, or apologize for his crimes—only telling the judge that he understood the charges and what the repercussions would mean before pleading guilty to the three murder charges.

Listening to Penton plead guilty was a bittersweet moment for Bradshaw. In December, his oldest daughter, Jodi, had been married in Italy. He and Gail and Laci had traveled to Rome for the wedding and visited the Vatican, as well as several churches. It was a beautiful wedding and wonderful trip; however, Bradshaw kept thinking about Penton and the upcoming trial. On his way out of the San Silvestre church, he noticed a small collections box. He took a coin out of his pocket and said a prayer that Penton would eventually confess his crimes. And now the bogeyman that he and Holleman had pursued all those years before was standing in front of a judge in a Collin County courtroom doing just that.

Tammy Lopez was the only family member of a victim to make a statement. Sweet was surprised at how composed she was, though, as was obvious from the first time he met her, she was not the same person she'd been before her daughter was murdered. There were few dry eyes in the courtroom, and even Penton wept—though he didn't so much as glance at her—when she looked at him and said that he didn't just murder her daughter, he'd killed part of her, too.

Later, when announcing the decision to accept the plea deal to the media, Collin County District Attorney John Roach said that when Penton pleaded guilty to three murder charges, he also waived all rights to file any motions for a new trial or appeal his sentence. Just six months after stating that his office would seek the death penalty, Roach now said his office had achieved the goal it set out for itself when Penton was indicted.

"We have permanently removed and separated a predator from the rest of us," he said. "This is not the first time, nor will it be the last, that the resources of my office have been deployed to ensure such a result."

Assistant district attorney Davis told various media sources that new evidence had come to light that could have created reasonable doubt in jurors' minds as to Penton's guilt. He said that the evidence was circumstantial but might have been enough to cause a juror to hesitate to convict.

"I have no doubt that if David Penton were found guilty in these cases he would have received the death penalty," he said. "The risk was on the guilt portion of this case."

An angry Mike Meeks, however, told the *Dallas Morning News* that he'd been led to believe that the meeting was to discuss jury selection. The plea deal was done before the families ever arrived at the courthouse, he said, and Davis *"didn't ask us"* if they wanted to accept. *"His words were, quote, 'I can't win this case.'"*

Then he told them about the deal. *"I feel like I have a right to be mad; I felt like we had all been lied to by Greg Davis."*

The plea bargain left Meeks saying he was confused as to whether the authorities had even arrested the right man for his daughter's murder. He asked why, if Penton wasn't in Texas when one of the girls was killed, would the prosecutors even accept an admission of guilt for the crime? And why would Penton plead guilty if he had the evidence to prove he was innocent?

The families deserved a trial to learn the answers to those and other questions, Meeks complained. *"For eighteen months, I've been told this man was going to die. I was told from Day One that this was a death penalty case. They're taking the easy way out, in my opinion."*

Asked by a reporter if he would have preferred a trial even if Penton was acquitted, Meeks didn't hesitate to answer yes. Now, he said he would have to file an open records request so that he could look at all of the evidence for himself. *"For the last 20 years—since January 19, 1985—I've been told this and that, but I've never been allowed to see anything. In the law's eyes it is over; I guess I need it to be over in mine."*

Meeks said he did have one regret about his actions. By walking out on the meeting with Davis, he wasn't there to face Penton in the courtroom later.

Tammy Lopez told the media that Penton showed no remorse at the hearing. *"He killed our children, but he also killed us,"* she said. *"He destroyed their lives, and he also destroyed our lives. And we're the ones paying."*

Sobbing as she described Penton to the media as *"a devil,"* she, too, said she wished that Penton had gone to trial and received the death penalty. Her only solace was that in the end, he would pay for his crimes on Earth and after his death. *"Because God knows what he did and he will be punished,"* she said. *"I know he's not going to go through the pain my daughter went through, but he's going to go through pain."*

Christie Proctor's mother, Laura, said that at least Penton would never harm another child. *"Essentially, he'll die in jail."* But the girl's father, Howard, added that while there was *"some sense of closure. I personally would have preferred the death penalty."*

One of Penton's defense attorneys, Gregg Gibbs, said he was pleased with the plea bargain. He said his client understood that he was never going to be a free man again. *"We just wanted to save his life,"* he told the *Dallas Morning News*. *"David is very ready to get out of the Collin County Jail. I know he is glad this is over; this brings closure to the family and to the client."*

Gibbs, a former Plano police detective before he left for law school, acknowledged that the new evidence was not *"rock solid or bulletproof."* However, he said, it would have improved his client's chances at trial.

Penton's other attorney, Edwin King, called the deal a *"fair resolution"* and said that the state's evidence was *"very thin."* He said the recent evidence discovered by the defense indicated that his client was working in Ohio at the time of the Reyes murder. The decision to accept the plea bargain was Penton's.

The "new evidence" the Penton defense team revealed on the eve of his trial turned out to be timecards that purported to show that the defendant was working for a temp agency in Ohio at the time of Roxann Reyes' abduction and murder. The timing was such that Sweet and the other detectives didn't have the opportunity to investigate the claim.

However, Sweet later looked into the defense claims. He learned that Penton had indeed worked for the temp agency, but one of his jobs was dealing with the timecards. The killer kept all the records for when temp agency employees, including himself, were working, so he could have easily manufactured an alibi.

The timecard pretext was flimsy at best, especially when confronted by the mountain of evidence Sweet and the other detectives had gathered. But debunking the defense ploy would have taken reopening the investigation, money and time away from his regular caseload for more trips to Ohio, and the cooperation of the temp agency to prove Penton manipulated his timecards to give himself an alibi. And with the trial only days away, it wasn't possible. The District Attorney had to make a decision and chose to make sure that Penton never left prison.

When Sweet heard about King's comments on the state's evidence, he shrugged it off as typical defense attorney posturing and thought they'd pulled a fast one. The defense knew it would be tough for the prosecution to investigate the "new evidence" before the trial. And if the defense really believed that the evidence was valid, why plead guilty at all?

However, it was over, at least for the three cases he and the other detectives had focused on. But that that didn't mean that Penton was off the hook for any other murders he'd committed. Before the child killer was shipped back to Ohio, the detectives asked the defense attorneys if they could talk to him again. They wanted to see how close they were with some of the details of their investigation and hear the truth from Penton himself.

So Billy Meeks set up a lunch meeting with King,

at which the defense attorney was very complimentary about their investigation. "Very thorough," he said. "You did a good job." But when they asked if they could interview his client again, he said no.

Why not, Sweet asked, Penton had forfeited any right to appeal the Texas conviction, so whatever he said in that regard couldn't come back to haunt him at a new trial there?

But King said he still couldn't allow it. He said he was worried that Penton might implicate himself in other murders, and the deal with the Collin County District Attorney was only for the three he pleaded guilty to at the hearing.

Sweet knew then that Sunnycalb was right about there being more murders. The defense attorney had as much as admitted that Penton had killed other children, and the attorney was protecting him from self-incrimination. But that didn't mean Sweet and the other detectives had to let it go.

PART III

Prayers Have Been Answered

CHAPTER TWENTY-THREE

Sweet was disappointed that Penton escaped the death penalty. He thought that of the cases he'd worked on in his life, no killer was more deserving. But also gone was the possibility of using it as leverage to get him to confess to other murders he'd committed and reveal where he'd left the remains.

However, he understood Davis's concern. It only took one holdout juror—someone basing their decision on emotion or some wacky theory, rather than the evidence—to ruin all the hard work they'd put into making Penton accountable for his crimes.

After Penton's hearing, Sweet had an opportunity to talk to Tammy Lopez in the hallway outside of the courtroom. She hugged the tall Texas lawman and said once again that she was grateful for his efforts. "I'll never forget what you did for me and Roxann."

When he got back to the office, Sweet called Tiffany Ibarra and told her about the plea bargain. She accepted the news, thankful that she wouldn't have to face Penton. Julia Diaz also seemed relieved when he talked to her. They were both satisfied that the bogeyman who'd terrified them as children and would haunt them the rest of their lives wasn't going to ever be free to kill or frighten anyone again.

Bruce Bradshaw was also okay with the deal, but for other reasons. Visiting the prison in Ohio was his first experience seeing what existence was like for a prisoner serving a life sentence. Every detail of the prisoner's life was monitored and scheduled. Small commodities, such as a can of soda or a candy bar, were a treasure to be hoarded or traded like gold. Prison was a dangerous world to live in, consisting of steel, concrete, and hard men, whom society had judged not fit for life in the community. He thought that spending every day and night for the rest of his life locked up behind walls and bars was a worse fate than execution, and Penton was welcome to it.

The deal that spared Penton's life also brought to a close a long dark chapter in Bradshaw's career. There had been times after Sweet arrived at his office and revived the pursuit of Penton that he wondered if they were just headed for another dead end. But whenever he felt like giving up, Sweet and Don Phillips kept him going, and he would always be grateful to them for that; together with Billy Meeks, they'd made a heck of a team and laid to rest a case he thought might never end.

Sweet stayed in contact with Sunnycalb, who continued to feed him information on other cases Penton had admitted. When he was working on the Texas murders, Sweet continuously had to keep Sunnycalb focused on them, promising that when his investigation was over, they'd pursue these others. So now when time allowed, Sweet took notes while talking to Sunnycalb and then passed on the information to law enforcement agencies where the crimes were committed. He also vouched for the informant's credibility.

Sunnycalb wasn't always cooperative. He didn't want to work with anyone except Sweet, who had to convince him to cooperate every time a detective from another agency wanted to talk to the inmate. It did not take a lot of explaining to convince Sunnycalb that the Garland Police Department was not going to let Sweet go all over the country working on cases, nor were other departments going to want him to poke his nose into their jurisdictions.

Sweet had his own current caseload to deal with, as well as a growing reputation as a cold case investigator, which included solving the 1992 murder of a 79-year-old woman and the shooting of her three grandchildren. The woman's son, a career criminal named Ron Adkins (aka Tyler), who had once been arrested in Memphis for attempting to steal the body of Elvis Presley, had stolen money from a drug dealer in Tennessee. Although Tyler tried to claim that the murder and shootings were tied to his work as an informant for various law enforcement agencies, the truth of the matter was that his own criminal actions resulted in the attack on his family. But Sweet was able to put together the case by tracking down old witnesses, including several who recanted original statements that backed up the killers' alibis, and put the two gunmen—one in 2007 and the other in 2011—in prison for life.

Sweet pursued many other violent men accused of murder and never lost a court case, but none of them compared in pure evil to Penton. In continuing to try to interest other law enforcement agencies to look into other cases against Penton, he hoped that one of those agencies would try to win a death penalty sentence. If Penton faced execution, Sweet believed that he might save his life by working out a deal to reveal what other murders he'd committed and help authorities find the remains.

Two of those cases Sweet pushed were in Texas. Early on in his discussions with Sunnycalb, the informant had told him that Penton talked about abducting and murdering Angelica Gandara in Temple, Texas. But when Sweet contacted the Texas Ranger assigned to the case, the man sent him his files and wished him luck. He'd since found out that the officer had been close to retirement and not interested in pursuing old cases.

After Penton pleaded guilty, Sunnycalb continued bringing up the Gandara case, and Sweet decided to find out what he could on the case. He learned that Angelica was eleven years old when she disappeared in her hometown of Temple, Texas, on the evening of July 14, 1985. She was walking home from her grandmother's house only two blocks away when she vanished. A witness claimed he saw the little girl in an unidentified pickup truck in the company of an unidentified Caucasian male and female. The witness said the dirty, beat-up truck's hood, front fender, and bed were painted red and white, the doors were blue and the top of the truck was white.

Although the vehicle didn't match any Penton was known to drive, nor was he known to commit his crimes with a female accomplice, Sweet still thought it was worth checking out. Temple was only twenty-five miles from Fort Hood, where Penton was stationed at the time. And Sunnycalb seemed to have a lot of details about the crime.

Sweet called The Temple Police Department. The Texas Ranger he'd contacted earlier in his investigation wasn't interested in solving an old cold case. But after Sweet explained why he was calling, Det. Jerry Bryan with the Temple Police Department jumped right in.

After speaking with Sunnycalb, the investigator told Sweet that the informant had discussed some details that he believed could have only come from someone who had been in the area or heard about from someone else who had. They knew that Sunnycalb had never been to

Temple, Texas, so he'd had to learn them from someone else.

However, Penton was not the only suspect. Temple police also considered a convicted rapist-murderer, Ramiro Rubi Ibarra (no relationship to Tiffany or her parents) as a possibility. In 1997, Ibarra was convicted of the 1987 rape and murder of a sixteen-year-old girl in the area. An acquaintance of the girl's family, he'd broken into the house and attacked her one night when she was alone. He'd been convicted in that case and sentenced to death. The police thought he also made a good suspect for the Gandara abduction, but were never able to link him to the case.

In the meantime, Sweet, Bradshaw, and Meeks traveled several times to Temple to help the investigators with their case. They even met with a team of FBI agents who were helping Bryan and showed them the PowerPoint demonstration Phillips and Meeks had put together for Davis. Soon after, Penton was declared a "person of interest."

Another case that Sunnycalb mentioned quite a bit over the years took more digging by Sweet because the informant didn't have a name or exact location. He said that Penton talked about abducting a young black girl from a mobile home in East Texas. "He brags about how he crawled in a window and took her out right past her parents' bedroom door, which was open," Sunnycalb said.

While still working on the Texas cases, Sweet looked up all the missing children cases from that time period. He found one that seemed to fit Sunnycalb's description in Big Sandy, Texas. On the night of April 2, 1986, five-year-old Ara "Niecie" Johnson was abducted from her bedroom in her mother's mobile home and never heard from again. She'd gone to bed that night dressed in a pair of panties and wrapped in an orange bedspread, which was also missing. Her mother discovered her gone in the morning and the front door left open.

Sweet called the police department in Big Sandy and asked for details about the crime and was told that the kidnapper gained entrance through a back window and left with the child through the front door. Once again Sunnycalb was right on the money. But when Sweet tried to interest the local law enforcement agencies, he never heard back.

Now, three years later, Sweet tried again by calling the Upsher County Sheriff's Office. This time he was put in touch with investigator Freddie Fitzgerald, whom he told about Sunnycalb and the role he'd played in solving the Dallas-area cases. "He can be difficult to work with, but he's worth listening to," he advised.

Perhaps because of his success with the Penton investigation, he could tell that Fitzgerald was taking him seriously. The investigator drove to Garland several times to look at Sweet's files and kept the Garland detective updated on the status of his investigation.

After that, the Upshur County Sheriff's Office was convinced they were after the right man. The sheriff, Anthony Betterton, told Kenneth Dean of the *Tyler Courier-Times-Telegraph* that Penton was now a "person of interest" in the Johnson abduction.

Of course, word got around in the Ohio prison system. Aware that other authorities were now investigating him because of Sweet's continued interest in cases, in March 2007 Penton granted his first interview since his conviction to Dean, who traveled to Ohio to meet with him.

In the story that followed, Dean described Penton

as *"intelligent, elusive, and somewhat proud of his 'notoriety.' He also contradicted himself numerous times. Penton's moods changed so quickly, the changes were sometimes unnerving to watch. As he answered some questions that clearly bothered him, he would become red-faced with anger as he moved his hands rapidly, then his eyes would tear up, and finally he would sneer or laugh in my direction. The changes often occurred within a one-minute period."*

Penton wouldn't discuss the Nydra Ross case with the reporter because of *"other investigations"* pending against him, particularly the 1986 disappearance of six-year-old Shannon Sherrill from Thorntown, Indiana. However, he denied murdering the three girls in Texas, even though he'd pleaded guilty. He told Dean, *"'I only signed the plea agreements because I would be sitting on death row right now in Texas, and here I might have a chance that someone will listen to me.'"*

According to Dean's story, Penton said he also pleaded guilty to spare his family from going through another murder trial. *"He blamed the crimes on a Jordanian national he says fled the country before authorities could interview him,"* Dean wrote. *"But, he said, 'If I had been on a jury if the Texas cases went to trial I would have convicted myself.'"* He also told the reporter that he would have convicted himself for the murder of Nydra Ross.

However, Penton said, police agencies and the FBI were conspiring against him in order to clear up old abduction cases across the country. *"'I'm not a monster,"* Dean quoted him saying, *"though I have been called a monster. But I didn't go around the country killing little kids.'* He did admit that while in Korea, he solicited prostitutes 'and some may have been underage.*

... It wasn't so much that I fancied the age as it was about cleanliness. I mean there were a lot of diseases out there.'"

Penton blamed his troubles on Sunnycalb and his other former cellmates, who, he said, were just trying to shorten their own prison sentences. When the reporter pointed out that Sunnycalb was still talking to authorities without getting a deal, Penton said it was because his former cellmate had a personal grudge against him.

When Sweet read the article, he wasn't surprised by Penton's claims that he was innocent of the Texas murders and only pleaded guilty to escape the possibility of the death penalty. Penton had never intentionally admitted to any of his crimes, from the death of his son to the murder of Nydra Ross; he was a habitual liar, and Sweet expected nothing else except more lies.

A month after Dean's interview with Penton appeared in the *Tyler Courier-Times-Telegraph*, the Upshur County Sheriff's Department announced that Penton was a "strong person of interest" in the abduction of Ara Johnson.

"From the information we are getting, we definitely need to talk to him," Upshur Det. Fitzgerald told Dean. *"We have to err on the side of caution, but this information brings hope to a case where hope was all but abandoned."*

While police investigators in Temple and Upshur counties had jumped in with both feet, Sweet didn't always meet with such enthusiasm. Not every law enforcement agency was willing to even look into the possibility of solving the cold case abduction and murder of a child. He contacted more than a dozen agencies—from Pennsylvania to Arkansas and Louisiana to Indiana and back to Texas—with what he thought was viable information from Sunnycalb. Only a few bothered to call him back, and even fewer did anything about it.

The case that drew Sweet in the most, however, was the October 5, 1986, disappearance of Shannon Sherrill in Indiana. In the fall of 2005, Sunnycalb called to express his frustration that no one seemed interested in his information about the Sherrill case. Having tried unsuccessfully, himself, to get the attention of law enforcement in Thorntown, Sweet suggested that Sunnycalb write a letter to the town marshal.

However, even that failed to get a response until one day in June 2006, Sweet received a telephone call from a reporter, Megan Durbak, with the *Kokomo Tribune*. She introduced herself and said she was working on a story about a 1986 case of a missing child, Shannon Sherrill. He started to pass her off to the Garland PD press information officer, but then something she said something that caught his attention.

Durbak said she was working on a story for the 20th anniversary of Shannon's abduction and was allowed to look at the Thorntown police file on the case. Lying on the very top was Sunnycalb's letter. "He said he knows who the killer is and that if they had any questions about his credibility, they should contact Det. Gary Sweet with the Garland Police Department in Texas," she explained. "Your phone number was in the letter."

Sweet talked to her for quite awhile and said that he believed that Sunnycalb had valid information. He told her that he'd tried to pass that information on to the Thorntown police several times without any results.

The next day, Sweet received another telephone call, this time from Jeff Heck, a lieutenant with the Indiana State Police. He, too, was looking into the Shannon Sherrill case and wanted to know about Sunnycalb.

CHAPTER TWENTY-FOUR

June 22, 2006

The afternoon that Heck called Sweet, the 27-year Indiana State Police veteran was nearing the end of his career. He'd been the sort of cop who believed that being a police officer was who you were, not what you did for a paycheck; that when something bad happened and someone needed to step forward and take responsibility to try to make it right, it would be him. They were traits he'd inherited from his father, who'd also been an Indiana State Trooper and detective, and Jeff had never wanted to be anything else.

Oh, there'd been some thought of going to law school, with encouragement from his father. Like any parent, Loyd Heck wanted his son to have it better than he did, perhaps with less trauma. He'd experienced the dangers of being a police officer, and in thirty-four years as a state police officer, he'd seen enough of the impact of crime to last a lifetime. That included being an investigator of the infamous Hollandsburg Massacre in which four young men, for no other reason than wanting to know what it was like to kill, broke into a mobile home in Hollandsburg, Indiana, on Valentine's Day in 1977 and executed four other young men, and critically injured their mother, with shotguns. But beginning in grade school, then high school, and college at DePauw University, Jeff had wanted to follow in his father's footsteps. Law school was only a fleeting consideration, and in 1978 he became an Indiana State Trooper.

Although he hoped to become a detective like his father, Jeff Heck had spent the first part of his career as a uniformed patrol officer working traffic and criminal complaints in Boone County, a "donut" county that surrounded the metropolitan area of Indianapolis. Bisected by Interstate 65, there was always plenty of activity, whether dealing with highway accidents or crimes.

In 1986, the year after Shannon Sherrill disappeared, he got his wish and was promoted to detective. Or, at least, he got part of his wish. While a uniformed trooper, he'd hoped to replace Francis Shrock when he retired as the detective in Boone County. He'd even dropped humorous "hints" by picking up applications at various employers in the region and putting them in the senior detective's mailbox. But Shrock was still going strong when an opening popped up at ISP headquarters in Indianapolis, so Heck took the job in the White Collar Crime Section.

For the next seven years, Heck worked mostly white collar crimes and specialty property crimes, drug trafficking, and auto theft, rising to the rank of sergeant. In 1994, he was promoted to lieutenant and commander of the special investigations unit. One of the units under his command was Crimes Against Children. The unit investigated complaints of physical and sexual abuse, eventually leading to the creation of a Cyber Crime Unit that dealt with the forensic examination and prosecution of child pornography.

However, the one case that stuck with him was the disappearance of Shannon Sherrill; nor had it ever been forgotten in Thorntown. Every year as the anniversary of the crime came around, or some other child disappeared, some reporter was bound to interview Mike Sherrill at the gas station he owned. He'd talk about how he still hoped that someday, somehow, his daughter would come home. Dorothy Sherrill also gave several interviews, but they seemed to take so much out of her that she appeared less and less in the media.

Every so often, there'd be a sighting, or someone would call claiming to have experienced a memory "flashback," or was feeling guilty that they hadn't called sooner. Or someone would hear someone boasting at a bar about knowing something related to the case. Psychics gained notoriety and a few minutes of fame in the media by claiming that they "knew" Shannon was still alive.

With each new claim or story, the tragedy would come alive all over again. Shannon's parents, including Mike's second wife, Becky, would get their hopes up, and then have to relive the pain and put it behind them again when the tips proved to be false or meaningless.

Town Marshal Campbell never got over it. He died young from multiple sclerosis; confined to a wheelchair before his death, he lamented that his biggest regret was not having solved Shannon's abduction.

Shrock, who'd headed up the Indiana State Police side of the investigation, retired in August 2001 still haunted by the tragedy. Other than his own father, Shrock and Boone County Sheriff Ern Hudson were Heck's greatest influences as a state police officer. Shrock was a hard worker, very dedicated and yet also very compassionate towards victims and suspects. Many of the leads that came in on the Sherrill case went directly to him because he was so well known in the county and had worked on the original investigation.

Hudson retired and moved to Colorado to work as an undersheriff in Larimer County. He, too, was troubled by the one case of a missing child that had never been solved. But there was nothing anyone could do; Shannon was gone, and her abductor remained an evil mystery.

The Sherrill case was a caveat on Heck's career. He'd had a great run, solved a lot of crimes—been that guy who stepped forward and took responsibility. However, there was a "but;" as in, he'd had a great career "but" wished they'd been able to find who took Shannon and bring her remains home to her family.

Then in July 2003, the case came roaring back into Heck's life when he got a call at home from Shrock. The retired detective said that the new Thorntown marshal had just reached out to him about a woman who claimed to be the long-lost Shannon Sherrill. The mystery woman had convinced Shannon's parents that she was legit.

The Thorntown marshal needed help, but it was a Sunday and no one else was available, Shrock said. He knew that Heck had been involved as a young trooper in the original investigation and, with every other law officer who'd been part of the investigation dead or gone, he'd turned to him.

As the commander of the Special Investigations Section, Heck didn't normally take on cases himself, but instead assigned them to one of his officers. This time, however, he decided to look into the woman's claims himself. If someone had asked him, Heck would have said he assigned himself to the case because there was no one else around that afternoon, and he didn't want to wait. The truth was that he was going to work the case no matter what.

Heck called the marshal, who relayed the story:

The day before, July 26, a woman who gave her name as Beth Ann Harris called Dorothy Sherrill and said, *"I think I might be Shannon."* She said she was calling from Virginia and had been in therapy when she suddenly began remembering things from her childhood in Indiana and being abducted.

A series of telephone calls flew back and forth between Shannon's parents and Harris and other people who said they were Harris' family. Harris had also called the marshal and other police agencies. Mike, Becky, and Dorothy were convinced; their daughter was back from the dead. Harris also called the national media, who picked up on the feel-good story and by Monday had arrived en masse in Thorntown, as well as in Lebanon, the Boone County seat, where television trucks with their big antennae crowded the courthouse square. The local press breathlessly reported that Harris' dental records, scars, and even a birthmark were all a match for the missing girl, though none of that was true.

Heck spoke to Harris and her relatives, and in spite of his initial skepticism, started to believe the story could be true. The woman seemed to recall some Indiana landmarks and even some personal items about the Sherrill family. Looking back, he would realize that he'd desperately wanted it to be true, and even when it started to go wrong, he held onto the hope that his suspicions, not Harris, were false.

However, by Monday afternoon Heck knew Harris was a charlatan. It became clear that like a sideshow fortune-teller, she'd gleaned little bits of information from the Sherrills, which she then turned around, as if the details were from her own memories. Then, in combination with information she'd found on the internet, she wove a convincing tale. She'd even used three different names and three voices to convince the Sherrills and investigators, including Heck, that they were speaking to her relatives.

As Heck's investigation continued, her story unraveled. She gave him a telephone number, a list of schools she'd attended, and even a Social Security number, none of which were real. He then traced her telephone calls back to an apartment in Topeka, Kansas, inhabited by a woman named Donna Walker.

Thirty-five years old, which was twelve more than Shannon would have been, Walker was already known to other law enforcement agencies, including the FBI, for other elaborate hoaxes, assuming other identities, and attempting to provide false information on other high-profile cases.

Assisted by the Topeka Police Department, Heck arranged for a warrant to have Walker arrested, all of which took several days. In the meantime, he got the Indiana State Police public information office to deflect some of the media attention. Although he wanted to tell the Sherrills what was going on, he hesitated. While he could count on Dorothy to stay quiet—in fact, sometimes she was criticized by the public for being "unemotional" because she declined to comment—he'd learned that what he told Shannon's father and Becky usually found its way to the media. With the national media camped out in Thorntown, he didn't want Walker to hear about her impending arrest and flee.

He was forced to reveal the truth when he learned from Dorothy that her two sisters were in their car and on the road to Virginia to "pick up Shannon." He had to tell her the truth, and then ask her to keep it quiet. She broke down and began to cry, but agreed that she'd keep the secret.

However, he still waited to tell Mike Sherrill. He didn't blame the man for doing whatever he felt was necessary after all he'd been through, but Heck couldn't take a chance. He then flew to Kansas, arrested Walker, and brought her back to Indiana. On the flight, she was chatty and seemed to think of it all as a big adventure.

The next day, Mike Sherrill arrived at the press conference expecting to hear that the investigation had confirmed that Harris was his daughter. He even hoped that she might be present at the press conference for an emotional reunion. Instead, the press information officer announced that that it had all been a cruel hoax and that Walker was in Indiana State Police custody. His hopes shattered, Shannon's father began to sob and collapsed on the floor.

Present at the press conference, Heck felt terrible for Shannon's father. He couldn't imagine the pain of having lost a child in such a way, or of having his hopes raised so high only to have them dashed. Although he believed the secrecy was necessary, he would always regret it.

Shannon's parents weren't Walker's only victims. Dorothy's mother was taken to the hospital complaining of chest pain when told it was a hoax. Also, at the same time she was pretending to be Shannon, Walker was telling a dozen young, childless couples, including an Indianapolis police officer and his wife, that she was a young pregnant woman who had chosen them to be the lucky adoptive parents of her baby. Their hopes, too, disappeared with the revelation that she was an imposter.

In retrospect it was difficult for Heck to understand why Walker created such elaborate, cruel hoaxes. She never asked for money—not from the Sherrills and not from the young couples. Walker's lawyer described her as a mentally ill woman who thought she was helping people by pretending their dreams were about to come true. But Heck had another theory; he acknowledged that Donna Walker might have some mental issues, but he also saw her as a bully who enjoyed causing other people pain.

Nor were strangers through hurting Dorothy. Shortly after the hoax was exposed, she appeared on the Montel Williams television show, where a psychic named Sylvia Browne told her that her daughter was still alive. The psychic claimed that Shannon had been brainwashed into believing that she was someone else's daughter and that Donna Walker might have more information about it than she'd revealed to police. Browne said it would all come out at the trial when Walker was questioned on the witness stand.

None of it, of course, was true. Walker didn't know anything more than she'd picked up on the internet and by winnowing details from the family. Nor did Browne. In fact, there was no trial. Walker pleaded guilty to felony attempted identity deception and misdemeanor false informing. She was sentenced to eighteen months in prison—a term Mike Sherrill described as "a slap on the wrist"—and four years probation. She served nine months and then returned to her home in Kansas.

The surprising thing was despite all the national publicity generated by the Walker case, the police did not receive a single new tip. What that told an experienced investigator like Heck was that the perpetrator was either dead or in prison. People talk; it's human nature, and sooner or later, he believed, the killer would have said something to someone who reported it.

After the Walker hoax, Heck stayed in touch with the Sherrills. He wanted to show them that their daughter was not forgotten and to give them a name and a face to turn to when they needed it. Most of his contact was with Dorothy. He'd gone out of his way with the media to let them know that her previous silence was at his request. But broken-hearted for a second time, she withdrew into what she told one reporter was a "big, old dark hole."

It was Mike who called Heck at home late on the night of June 21, 2006 and wanted to know "what are you going to do about that letter?"

"What letter?" Heck asked, confused.

The Thorntown marshal's office had a letter that said an Ohio prison inmate had information about Shannon's disappearance, Sherrill said.

"How do you know about it?"

A reporter with the *Kokomo Tribune* named Megan Durbak had seen the letter, along with an amateur private investigator from Maine named Mark Harper, who'd volunteered his services to Mike Sherrill. Heck was skeptical, but he said he'd look into it.

The next day, Heck drove to Thorntown and met with the marshal, who showed him the letter Durbak and Harper had seen in the file. Written on November 29, 2005, it was from an Ohio inmate named Jeffrey Sunnycalb. As Mike Sherrill had said, Sunnycalb claimed to have information about Shannon's disappearance and said that a Texas detective named Gary Sweet could vouch for him.

That afternoon, Heck called Sweet and talked to him at length about Sunnycalb and the cases in Texas. His skepticism disappeared. The delay in the contents of the letter being investigated would later cause the town marshal to be harshly criticized in the media, and even issue an apology to the family. But in the meantime,

Heck was back on the case.

Five days later, Heck drove to the Warren Correctional Facility in Ohio to speak to Sunnycalb. Again, working cases was not his responsibility, plus he was less than a year from retirement. But the fact that he lived Lebanon, had worked the area as a trooper, participated in the original investigation into Shannon's' disappearance, and taken the lead in the Donna Walker case made him the logical choice to pursue this lead. He also felt an obligation to work the case—that he owed it to Shrock, Hudson, and Campbell. It felt like he was carrying the torch for the other lawmen for whom their careers were marred by the "but" that was the Sherrill case. He was honored to do it; there was simply no way he was going to let someone else work the case.

Heck didn't tell Sunnycalb that he was coming. When the inmate was pulled into a small interview room, he was leery and worried that other inmates would find out he was talking to a cop. Like two poker players, neither the informant nor the detective wanted to show their hands. It was obvious to Heck that Sunnycalb had an end game and wasn't willing to talk in detail until he'd figured out how to get what he wanted. He said enough to interest Heck, but the detective also wanted to make sure the tail wasn't wagging the dog.

After leaving the prison, Heck called Megan Durbak and asked if she would hold the story while he looked into it. She agreed, and he then spent the next couple of weeks gathering as much information as he could, especially talking to Sweet. He wanted to know Penton's patterns, as well as what other inmates had said that tied the killer to Thorntown, Indiana, and Shannon Sherrill.

Then on July 6, Heck traveled back to the prison in

Ohio to speak to former police officer and current inmate Tim Creighton. Where Sunnycalb had let him know that he didn't appreciate him showing up unannounced, Creighton couldn't have been more cooperative.

By the time they were done, Heck was convinced that Creighton, who'd brought notes he'd made of his conversations with Penton, was credible. Penton had described specific areas of Thorntown—a creek, a railroad overpass, a hidden drive, and gate—that could have only come from someone who'd been there. Then Creighton picked Shannon's photograph out of a lineup; he said Penton had once had another picture of the girl in their cell.

One of Creighton's notes referred to Penton saying he'd disposed of Shannon's body in a large park area in southern Indiana by throwing her off a cliff into a ravine. Heck led a large search party to search the area, and though they found a cliff and ravine that matched the description, it was a large area and no remains were located. Nor were there any reports of unidentified remains having been located in that area when he checked with the local coroner's office, the sheriff, and local police, as well as the state natural resources department.

Heck spent the summer going back and forth between Indiana and Ohio to speak with Sunnycalb and Creighton, as well as accepting collect calls from them. Some of the inmates the Texas detectives interviewed were out of prison, so he had to go find them, particularly Howard Guiher and Tony Baker.

He also went back and reviewed the original case file on Shannon's abduction, personally checking out some of the leads that had been called in over the years. One person even insisted that Shannon had been run over by a drunk or unlicensed driver, who then panicked and buried her alongside of the road. It was a long shot, but Heck brought in cadaver dogs, specially trained to find bodies, but they didn't hit on a scent.

The most interesting information in the files was two reports from witnesses who claimed to have seen a suspicious white van in town that they knew didn't belong to any of their neighbors. Heck knew from Sweet that Penton had once owned such a vehicle, and indeed had been driving a white van when he murdered Nydra Ross. One of the witnesses had passed away, but Heck located the other and showed him photographs of white vans, including Penton's. The man shook his head, he couldn't be sure if one of them was the van he'd seen on that sunny day almost exactly twenty years earlier, but maybe.

Sunnycalb had also told Heck that when Penton was arrested for Nydra's murder, a pair of little girl panties had been found in the van. Those panties, Penton told him, had belonged to Shannon Sherrill. Heck called the Columbus Police Department and talked to Det. David Morris, who had worked on the Ross case. Again, Sunnycalb's information was good. The Columbus PD had a record of panties found in the van and even a photograph of them. Unfortunately, the underwear had been lost or destroyed, so there was no chance of testing for DNA.

Morris sent the photograph to Heck, which he put together in a "lineup" of photographs of panties and showed them to Dorothy Sherrill. She ruled out most of them. However, she said, the pair found in Penton's car was similar to the type Shannon would have worn, though she couldn't be sure what her little girl wore that day.

Heck also sent blood samples from Shannon's parents to the DNA lab in Texas that had tested the stained rags found in the attic of Penton's former home in Columbus. But there was no match.

In October, Heck traveled to Texas to meet up with Sweet, Bradshaw, Phillips, and Bryan. They spent most of a week going over the files for the Texas murders, looking for anything to connect Penton to Indiana. But other than the interviews with several inmates who said he'd talked about being in that state—some of it detailed enough that he believed it to be credible—there wasn't much new.

Then in November, Heck returned to the Warren Correctional Facility, where he sat down with Sunnycalb for one last interview. Although the inmate hesitated, he eventually cooperated when the detective said he wanted to tape the conversation.

On January 21, 2007, Heck flew to Oklahoma to interview Penton's former brother-in-law. The Mesquite detectives had told him about what the man said about driving around with Penton fantasizing about raping and killing young girls. The man was cooperative and acknowledged what he told Phillips was true, but said that his involvement in Penton's deviant behavior was all just talk and fantasy. He denied having participated in any actual abductions, including Shannon's, and passed a lie detector test.

Finally, there was only one thing left to do, and that was to talk to the bogeyman himself. On February 4, 2007, Jeff Heck found himself sitting in a motel room in Toledo, Ohio. Outside, it was snowing while inside on the television the Indianapolis Colts were playing the Chicago Bears in the Super Bowl in Miami, Florida. However, his mind wasn't on the game or the weather, but on the fact that the next day he'd be talking to the man he believed abducted and murdered Shannon Sherrill.

Heck knew there was no point in appealing to Penton on an emotional level. A psychopath wasn't going to care about giving "closure" for Shannon's parents by telling the truth and revealing where he'd left her body. The only person David Penton cared about was David Penton. So Heck was going to have to appeal to the monster's self-interest.

One advantage he had was that Penton didn't know he was coming. He wanted to be better prepared for the confrontation than the psychopath he was about to meet. He also didn't want to give Penton the opportunity to say no to the interview. Or if he did, he was going to have to say it face-to-face, and Heck wanted to meet him first. Up to that point, Penton was only a photograph; seeing him in the flesh would make the bogeyman real.

They were brought together in an interview room off of Penton's cellblock. After introducing himself and why he was there, Heck noted that Penton struggled for a moment so as not to appear surprised but quickly gathered himself.

The detective didn't waste any time beating around the bush. "I know you did it," he said. "And you know you did it. Let's get this thing closed. I can't get you drunk, or get you dope, or get you laid, but if you'll show us where you dumped or buried the body, maybe there's something I can do for you."

Heck said he'd talked to the Boone County prosecutor and could offer the one thing he knew Penton valued: his life. If he'd admit to the murder and helped find Shannon's remains, they wouldn't pursue the death penalty. He'd even brought a letter to that effect signed by the Boone County prosecutor, Todd Meyer.

The detective pointed out to the killer that he was treating him with respect. Prison inmates don't have much, so respect was something they clung to. It wasn't easy to stomach. Heck had to pretend to treat him as an equal, when what he wanted to do was push his head through the bars of a cell. Instead, he noted that rather than do things that could have made life more difficult—such as have him transported to the Boone County jail, where he wouldn't have his television, commissary, nearby relatives to visit him, yard time, his friends, and the safety of being kept in protective custody—he'd taken it easy on him.

Penton, of course, knew that Heck was playing a part. Still, he appreciated it enough to talk to the detective for three hours. He acted like they were just a couple of guys sitting down to talk. During that time, he admitted that he had a "taste for young girls." But he denied murdering Shannon Sherrill, or any of the others for which he'd been convicted. He was obviously trying to "sell" Heck on the idea that he was just this unfortunate, misunderstood guy, who hadn't committed the crimes he'd been accused of doing.

It was difficult to sit across from Penton, knowing what he'd done and listen to his lies. But what bothered Heck more was the man's arrogance. Penton was smug when he answered the questions he knew the detective was going to ask, and his facial expressions didn't match his protestations of innocence. He'd talk about the crimes in Texas, but always in general terms and didn't refer to the three girls by name. They were just "things" to him.

Finally, Heck thought he'd gone about as far as he was going to with Penton. Short of the threat of a trial, the killer wasn't going to cooperate. It wasn't just the possibility of the death penalty that would make him talk, either, though certainly Penton would do whatever it took to protect his miserable life. Heck realized there was something else at play.

Penton was "institutionalized." He wasn't suffering in prison; he'd accepted that he was never getting out and had everything he wanted or needed to be comfortable in his incarcerated life. He had a television, food, shelter, friends, and a social life. His relatives visited and put money in his prison account.

However, all of that would be messed up if he was indicted in another state. He'd be moved from his comfortable surroundings to a place he didn't know, such as a county jail—which would be like stepping down from the Hilton to a fleabag motel. If he was convicted in another state, he'd be starting all over in the pecking order, without friends and his established comfortable routine. Nor could his family visit as easily. And if sentenced to death somewhere, he'd be confined to a tiny cell on Death Row, twenty-three hours a day, without contact with the other inmates.

Penton liked to boast about his crimes to his fellow inmates. But unlike some serial killers, who enjoy the notoriety once they know they're not getting out again, Heck realized that Penton was concerned that more publicity might lead to being prosecuted again. He wasn't going to admit anything to cops or the media.

Heck knew that Penton was worried, even if he didn't talk, mostly about DNA evidence. The science had been in its infancy when he was abducting and murdering little girls in the 1980s, but it since had grown into a major crime-fighting tool. *He's afraid there's something out there that could convict him,* he thought.

"Well," Heck said, as the guard appeared to lead Penton back to his cellblock. "I hope to see you soon." He hesitated then asked. "Would you prefer to drive or fly back to Indiana?"The dig was intentional. He wanted Penton to be thinking about him as much as Heck had thought about the murderer. He hoped that he would be Penton's bogeyman.

As Heck left the Ohio prison, he felt exhausted. Like most officers after an important interview, such as the one he'd just conducted, there was always an adrenaline dump, followed by a tendency to second-guess what he'd said or left out. He worried until he later read a transcript of the interview and felt he'd covered all the bases. There was one thing he was now absolutely certain of: David Penton abducted and murdered Shannon Sherrill.

When he got back to Indiana, Heck met with Mike and Dorothy Sherrill and showed them a photograph of Penton. "This is the man I believe took your daughter," he said. He felt they deserved that, whether Penton was ever prosecuted for it or not; he hoped it brought them some relief.

He also updated retired ISP detective Shrock and former Sheriff Ern Hudson about the case. They'd been a good sounding board for him as he pursued the case against Penton and felt that they deserved to know. Their lives, too, were impacted by the abduction of Shannon Sherrill.

On March 15, 2007, Lt. Jeff Heck of the Indiana State Police forwarded his case to the Boone County Prosecutor's Office. He realized that it was a circumstantial case, and only a fair one at that. The main problem with it from his vantage point was that he'd been unable to put Penton in Indiana, except through statements made by the other inmates, and a former girlfriend of Penton, who told him that he'd been ticketed for speeding in the state, a claim he couldn't substantiate. But he felt, in his experience, that it was a case that could be won.

Still, it was Meyer's call. Meyer had prosecuted Donna Walker and knew the Sherrill case well. And his decision was that there wasn't enough to go forward with the case ... yet.

The day after Heck turned in the case was his last on the job. He respected Meyer's decision. It wasn't an open-and-shut case, but he'd done all he felt he could for Shannon Sherrill and her family, his fellow officers, and his community. Otherwise, he didn't think he would have been able to leave.

After filing the case with Meyer and retiring, Heck didn't want Penton to think he'd forgotten about him. So that year for every holiday and special occasion— Easter, Mother's Day, Father's Day, Halloween, and Christmas—he bought cards and sent them to the prisoner with small messages such as: "See you soon."

The cards had the desired effect. After receiving a Christmas card from Heck, Penton contacted a lawyer who wrote and demanded that the retired officer stop. Apparently, it frightened the murderer of little girls to know that he wasn't forgotten or forgiven.

EPILOGUE

David Elliot Penton cast the shiny pebbles of the young lives he took into the foul dark pond and devastated so many others who were overtaken by the spreading horror of what he did. Thanks to lawmen in Texas and Ohio, four families at least know the truth and have the remains of their children to mourn over. But a cold gravestone is scant solace for the warm love of a child and the joy of watching her grow into a young woman. There will always be those reminders—the birthdays, the photographs, that face in the crowd, a voice on a playground—that tug at the heart and bring on the tears.

Other families still wait, wondering if the bogeyman will ever reveal all of his crimes and the locations of his victims' bodies. Or will he carry his secrets to the grave with him and only answer to a higher power, not just for murders, but for the anguish he could have ameliorated by simply telling the truth.

These families can hope, perhaps, that charges will be brought against Penton for one of the other pending cases. Then, faced with the death penalty or with being moved from his comfortable life in an Ohio prison, maybe he will talk.

It could be just a small piece of evidence that tips the scales enough to encourage a prosecutor to move forward. For instance, on the back of one of the photographs seized from Penton's cell depicting a gray sedan, he'd written "Monrovia, packed for Texas."

When he saw the inscription, Sweet thought Monrovia might be a person's name. What he didn't know was that there is a town called Monrovia in Indiana, less than an hour's drive due south of Thorntown, where Shannon Sherrill disappeared. Unaware of the possible connection, Sweet didn't show the photograph to Jeff Heck, whose case lacked for being able to place Penton in Indiana. That possibility was noted recently, but it is not yet determined what effect, if any, it might have on the case.

In the meantime, the ripples continued to spread after Penton pled guilty to the three Texas murders. On July 10, 2011, Tiffany Ibarra died of a drug overdose. Even though Penton told her to get out of his van that day in 1986, in some ways the bogeyman never let her go. It wasn't just the terror he imposed on her personally. There was also survivor's guilt, knowing that just a few days later, on the same street, one of her schoolmates, Christie Proctor, suffered the fate he'd intended for Tiffany.

For twenty-five years, Tiffany saw his face and heard his voice in her nightmares. Yet, she had twice summoned the nerve to identify him to police detectives, and bravely prepared to face him in court. Doing so, she exhibited far more courage than the vile and evil creature who took her innocence, then murdered another little girl in her place. But while he continued to exist at taxpayer expense, eat warm meals, watch television, and regale his fellow inmates with his tales of horror, she had to live within the prison he created in her mind.

She was not alone in that prison. Tammy Lopez died in her sleep January 9, 2013, never having recovered from the abduction and murder of Roxann. For fourteen years, she'd held out hope that the remains found in the field near Murphy, Texas, weren't her daughter's. She wanted to believe that her husband kidnapped their child and took her to Mexico, where she was alive and happy.

However, the pebble that Penton tossed into the pond of her life overtook her. First, the necessities of Sweet's investigation forced her to face the reality of Roxann's brutal murder. She then waited for the case against *"the devil"* to be made and charges brought so that he would be exposed in a court of law for the beast that he is … only to lose her day in court when the Collin County District Attorney's Office made a strategic decision to ensure the killer would never leave prison, rather than gamble on his execution.

After his confession and guilty plea, there had been some degree of satisfaction, knowing that Penton had been forced to admit that he was a monster. But then, he'd torn Tammy's wounds open again, claiming in a newspaper article that he'd only pleaded guilty to avoid a possible death sentence.

Tammy moved back to her mother's property in Ohio, where she'd grown up. She stayed in a small mobile home in front of her mother's house, where she lived quietly, visiting with her mom, two daughters, and six grandchildren, planting flowers around the home, and mourning the child who was taken from her.

Although a type II diabetic with health issues, Tammy's death was unexpected. The coroner ruled "natural causes," but her mother believes that she died of a broken heart.After Penton's sentencing, Sweet called Joyce and told her about how well Tammy held it together when she spoke in court. "She wasn't the broken person she'd been for years," Joyce recalls. But the strength didn't last long, and when Tammy's husband, Jesus, died in November 2012, Joyce believes, "she didn't have anything left to live for."

All Joyce has left are the photographs of her daughter and granddaughter, and the pain. "Sometimes, I wish a day could go by in my life when I don't have to think about what happened to Tammy and Roxann."

Still, she says, the family will be forever grateful to Sweet, who she still hears from occasionally. She understands that the investigation took its toll on him and the other detectives, too. "In a way, they were all victims of David Penton."

As for Penton, Joyce wishes he'd received the death penalty. "I think he deserves it, but one way or the other, he better be worrying about God."

As a society, we rarely think about the impact of the ripples caused by a David Penton on detectives and their families. Except for the reported instance of unique bravery or sacrifice, usually the only stories we hear about law enforcement are those in which one bad apple defines the vast majority in the barrel. But as Joyce Davis noted, there are the police officers who invest their hearts, minds, souls, and sometimes health trying to bring the bogeyman to justice.

Indiana State Police detective Shrock died in 2008. There was some satisfaction for Jeff Heck that his mentor had lived long enough to be convinced that Penton was Shannon's killer and that he'd never be free to hurt another little girl. But "charged and convicted" is the measure of a detective's success, and that has not yet happened in the Sherrill case.

In the years since Heck left the ISP, nothing much has been done to move the case forward.In October 2009, his files were given to an ISP cold case detective. At the time, prosecutor Meyer told the media that there were several "persons of interest" in Shannon's disappearance, including Penton. The prosecutor was complimentary about Heck's investigation. *"He's done an excellent job of putting together the investigation."* But, he said, his office was at the same place regarding pursuing charges as it had been in 2007. *"There is no smoking gun. I hate to say it, but it's still a mystery to us."*

Mike Sherrill said in the same story that he wasn't sure what the cold case team would accomplish. *"Lt. Heck worked on the case for a whole year. I don't know what (they) can do than what he did. ... All we can do is hope. I just want to bring her home."*

As of the writing of this book, Heck's case file on Shannon Sherrill's disappearance remains in limbo, as do the cases in Temple and Upshur County, Texas. Those families must continue to wait for the answers; those murdered children await justice that has been delayed overly long.

As much as other detectives and their families were victims, too, of Penton, none paid a steeper price than Bob Holleman and those who loved him. As his ex-wife Molly Robertson notes, when he walked out of the door of his home on January 19, 1985, he never came back whole again.

After his retirement from the Mesquite Police Department, Holleman continued attending classes at various colleges. That included talking Southern Methodist University into creating a Ph.D. program in forensic anthropology, for which he was the first (and at the time, only) student. SMU also gave him a full-ride scholarship for his studies. But he only lasted a year, sometimes living out of a car while attending classes.

Later, he attended Columbia University in New York to study writing and even had a book contract.

However, he never finished the book.

By the time Penton was arrested, Holleman looked like a skinny bum, with long, stringy hair and no teeth. He had his pension check to live on, but he stayed in motels and his car. When Molly asked him why he wouldn't use the money to lease an apartment and have a regular roof over his head, he replied that at least living in a motel he would have some human interaction every time he paid for his room. He feared sinking so low into depression that he'd never walk out of the door otherwise.

"I don't have any friends," he told her. *"You're the only one who would check on me."* He didn't want to die alone, he said, and his body not be found for days.

Several times, Molly and her second husband took him in, once for nearly a year. She never spoke poorly of him to their children; her regret was that they never got to meet the man she'd married as they got older— the respected detective, the brilliant thinker he had been before The Call. They've only heard about *that guy*. They knew he was smart, and there were times when he seemed "normal," but that only made his downward spiral harder to take. He and his son, Michael, who couldn't forgive him for "throwing his life away" and not being there for the family, were estranged. Emily tried to hold on to the few memories she had and struggled to understand.

Bob certainly had his own regrets. He only went out on one date after he and Molly divorced; she knew that he longed for his family.

However, his greatest disappointment was failing to catch a killer. Even years after he retired from the police department, he confessed to Molly that he still scanned faces in crowds, looking for the man in the police artist sketch. Or he'd see a car and follow it. He knew it didn't make sense, but he couldn't let go.

Molly heard that Christi's killer was caught when a police officer from Mesquite called looking for Bob, who was living in Tennessee to be near his mom and brother. When she asked the officer why he was trying to find her ex-husband, he told her about Penton's indictment and arrest. She gave him a telephone number for Bob, but asked that he not mention that he'd told her the news first.

The next day, the telephone rang. When she answered, Molly heard a faint voice say, "It's over." She didn't recognize the voice at first and asked, "What's over?"

"They got him," said the voice, stronger now. "It's over."

The voice, Bob's voice, grew more confident. It was the voice that had been missing for so many years. "They got him. David Penton. They finally got that sorry son of a bitch. Are you hearing me? Christi's killer ... Bradshaw arrested Christi Meeks' killer!"

Then they both cried. So much pain. So much suffering. So many lost years, black times, and missed opportunities caused by the stone Penton tossed into the pond of their lives.

When they stopped crying, Bob told her that Penton was the suspect they'd looked at so many years before but could never make a case against. He said he was happy that Penton would never be able to hurt anybody else's kid or destroy another family. "I hope Christi can finally rest in peace."

However, there was one thing that bothered him. He was hurt that no one had told him what was going on during the investigation. "I lost everything because of that motherfucker," he said. "But I have to find out like I was some schmuck who wasn't there." He sighed and let it pass. He wasn't a cop anymore; they'd caught the bogeyman, and that was what mattered.

Shortly after that, Bob Holleman dropped by Bradshaw's office in Mesquite. His former partner had not seen him in several years and was shocked by his appearance. He seemed nervous, and when Bradshaw invited him to sit down, he fidgeted and appeared uncomfortable.

Bradshaw was prepared to have a lengthy discussion and tell him everything about the case, but Holleman only wanted to know two things. "Is this really the guy?" he asked. "And what did we miss back then?"

Assuring him that Penton was guilty beyond any doubt, Bradshaw said it was no fault of theirs that they had not been able to place Penton in Dallas. He explained about the Ohio inmates and other witnesses who had come forward, which, combined with the rest of the evidence gathered during the investigation, led to Penton pleading guilty. Holleman listened quietly and then got up and left without saying goodbye. Bradshaw never saw or heard from him again.

Eventually, Holleman moved to Mississippi to live near his brother, John, who'd moved after their mother passed away and took a position at "Ole Miss." One Sunday in November 2013, Bob called his brother and said he wasn't feeling good. However, when John asked if he wanted to go to the hospital—Bob could be something of a hypochondriac—he said no, he thought he'd wait to see if he felt better by the next day. But he asked his brother to check on him.

John called Monday afternoon but didn't get an answer. Nor did Bob pick up that night. When his brother still hadn't heard from him Tuesday, November 12, John went to check on him and found Bob lying on a bare mattress on the floor of his living room. He was dressed as if he intended to go out and looked like he was sleeping. But Bob Holleman had died as he feared he would, alone and undiscovered.

Molly was at work when she got the call from her daughter, Emily. "Daddy's dead." She didn't believe what she was hearing and made her daughter repeat herself. Even then, she still didn't want to believe it. Bob had been off drugs for two months and seemed to be doing well, more like his old self. She'd even received several jokes from him via text messages in the weeks prior to this, as well as the news that he was moving back to Texas.

"Don't worry, you won't have to put me up," he'd laughed. She could hear in his voice, even before he told her, that he was feeling better than he had in a very long time. It gave her hope that their son, Michael, could forgive him and finally have a positive relationship with his father. But it was not to be. The damage done by The Call had been too much to overcome.

Emily and her husband, Scott, drove from Nashville to Oxford, Mississippi, to take care of her father's final arrangements. Gathering his personal belongings, she was both amazed and deeply saddened that other than a few articles of clothing and random dishes, everything he owned fit into one box. She had her father cremated and his ashes placed in two urns.

Molly found it ironic and fitting that Emily brought her daddy's remains back to Texas in January 2014, twenty-nine years almost to the day that Christi Meeks disappeared. Emily gave one urn to Michael and kept the other for herself. She also separated some ashes and along with her brother and mother, their husbands, and Molly's mom and dad released them to the gentle breeze that blew over the graves of Bob's parents.

As Molly had noted many years earlier, some detectives who dedicated parts of their lives to tracking down the killer of little girls were better able than her husband at putting the tragedy on a shelf. But not so high on the shelf that the ripples didn't affect them, too, although sometimes only those closest to them know just how much it hurt.

Julie Sweet was relieved when after four years of consuming their lives, Penton pleaded guilty. Her husband can't rest when working on a murder case— sometimes sleeping only a couple of hours a night, if that—and she'd worried about the effect on his health.

The Reyes case seemed like it would never end, and that her husband might never again get a good night's sleep. She was proud of what he accomplished, and of all his cases, it was the most satisfying to his heart. His dogged pursuit of a monster did have an impact on their family; their girls probably suffered a little because of a dad who'd seen too much and was maybe a tad over-protective. But they always knew he loved them and understood that if they didn't have some of the freedom their friends did, it was because of what had happened to those other little girls.

When the decision was made to accept Penton's guilty pleas, Julie knew that her husband was disappointed. The case had affected him more than most. As a father, he'd identified with the murdered children and their families. He'd wanted Penton to be tried in a court of law, for the truth to come out in public, and for him to get the death penalty. Still, he'd told her once that if he could just put Penton away forever, knowing that he'd never get out and harm another child, then he could retire and know he'd had a good career.

When Sweet works on a cold case now, he makes sure that he contacts the families of the victims. By and large, they seem happy that he's at least making an effort; even if nothing comes of it, they appreciate that someone still cares. He still keeps Roxann's inspiration notebook on his desk, as well as the file for the Keith Calloway murder, to remind him that no matter how long it takes, the victims wait for justice, and the people who love them deserve answers. They deserve to know what happened, to recover the remains if possible, and know that the monster will not devastate some other family again.

In March 2006, Bruce Bradshaw retired from the Mesquite Police Department after 29 years of service. He'd promised Gail that after he found the person responsible for Christi's death, he would leave the department. Far too many hours, even days, had been spent away from home working child abuse and homicide cases. She'd never complained, nor had his children. But now with Jodi and Laci out of the house, Gail would be alone at home, and that wasn't fair.

However, he wasn't quite ready to leave law enforcement entirely. Shortly before he put in for his retirement, his elderly mother and other relatives let him know that the position of police chief in Comanche was open. It was a chance to return to his roots and be near his mother. After talking it over with Gail, he applied for the position and got the job.

When he thinks about Penton now, he's reminded of a traditional cowboy song he loved when he was growing up called, *Tying Knots In The Devil's Tail*. It's about two cowboys who, after a night of drinking in town, are accosted by the devil on their way back to the ranch. Of course, they do what any good cowboys will and lassoed, then branded the devil, after which they tied knots in his tale. The last verse of the song ends:

"So if you're ever up there in the Sierra Peaks
and you hear one helluva wail
It's just the devil a-yellin' about
them knots tied in his tail."

"I always thought of Penton as Satan," Bradshaw says. "But we had finally tied a knot in his tail, and he's still hollering about it."

In the spite of the stones Penton tossed in the pond, ending some lives and ruining others, evil did not ultimately triumph. But better than anything this author can write, the final words of this story—words that apply to so many others—come from Gail Bradshaw.

"We celebrate life with our daughters, enjoying every day experiences, looking forward to the future, working to fulfill dreams. We help them grow with the understanding that evil may exist, but faith and family are always there to support you. You never take each other for granted.

"The death of Christi and an armed robbery taught us to cherish each other and all life has to offer. Our family grew, and continues to grow, strong through faith. Christi will always be a part of our family. The robbers are in prison. Penton has confessed. Christi can rest. Prayers have been answered."

For More Bogeyman Photos

http://wildbluepress.com/BM-gallery

Use this link to sign up for advance notice of Steve Jackson's Next Book:

wildbluepress.com/AdvanceNotice

Word-of-mouth is critical to an author's long-term success. If you appreciated this book please leave a review on the Amazon sales page:

wildbluepress.com/8m99

Other WildBlue Press Books
by Steve Jackson

Smooth Talker

http://wbp.bz/st

No Stone Unturned

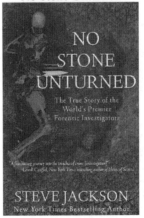

http://wbp.bz/nsu

**More True Crime You'll Love
From WildBlue Press.**

Learn more at: http://wbp.bz/tc

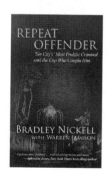

www.WildBluePress.com

More Mysteries/Thrillers You'll Love From WildBlue Press.

Learn more at: http://wbp.bz/cf

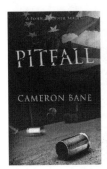
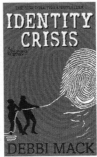
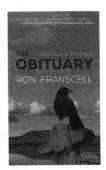

www.WildBluePress.com

Go to WildBluePress.com to sign up for our newsletter!

By subscribing to our newsletter you'll get *advance notice* of all new releases as well as notifications of all special offers. And you'll be registered for our monthly chance to win a **FREE collection of our eBooks and/or audio books** to some lucky fan who has posted an honest review of our one of our books/eBooks/audio books on Amazon, Itunes and GoodReads.

**Let Someone Else Do The Reading.
Enjoy One Of Our Audiobooks**

Learn more at: http://wbp.bz/audio

**Please feel free to check out more True CRIME
books by our friends at**

www.RJPARKERPUBLISHING.com

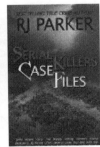
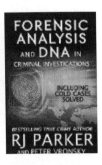

BOGEYMAN